TUESDAY'S CHILD

TUESDAY'S CHILD

HOW AMERICA CHOOSES ITS PRESIDENTS

BRIAN CHURCH

AMBERLEY

To Rev. Ed and Lib Hammersla,
Thank you for being my America

First published 2021

Amberley Publishing
The Hill, Stroud
Gloucestershire, GL5 4EP

www.amberley-books.com

Copyright © Brian Church, 2021

The right of Church, Brian to be identified as the Author
of this work has been asserted in accordance with the
Copyrights, Designs and Patents Act 1988.

British Library Cataloguing in Publication Data.
A catalogue record for this book is available from the British Library.

ISBN 978 1 3981 0193 7 (paperback)
ISBN 978 1 3981 0194 4 (ebook)

Typeset in 11pt on 13.5pt Sabon.
Typesetting by SJmagic Design Services, India.
Printed in the UK.

CONTENTS

Tuesday, Tuesday

At noon on Wednesday 20 January 2021, the candidate backed by calendar-conscious Americans on the first Tuesday after the first Monday in November will become President of the United States – if they get the oath right. If not, they'll do it again the next day (see 'Oathmeal' in Chapter 2).

Elected to near-universal surprise in 2016 on a pledge to 'Make America Great Again', U.S. President Donald Trump modestly sought to 'Keep America Great' in 2020 amidst all the challenges posed by the coronavirus pandemic. Republican Party candidate Trump faces former Vice President Joe Biden, the Democratic Party challenger, on Tuesday 3 November 2020 in what is expected to be a delightfully dirty campaign. The winner will be sworn in as president for four years in Washington, D.C. The 59th presidential election will have been the most watched political fight of all time inside the United States and around the world. Trump will like that.

Unless he loses.

Time to Concentrate

There is one overall winner, yes, but it's not a direct election where the triumphant presidential candidate is necessarily the one who gets the most votes nationally on Election Day. There are actually separate contests in the 50 different states along with the capital, Washington, D.C.[1] These 51 races, 51 results and 51 varying prizes collectively make up the Electoral College, America's mysterious way of choosing its presidents since the first election in 1789.

The prize on offer in each of the 51 races is a number of 'electoral votes' which can vary from state to state. Trump and Biden need to gather 270 electoral votes out of the 538 available to give them a winning majority overall on the Electoral College scoreboard. How to reach 270? Like Sheldon in *The Big Bang Theory* working out the order in which he'd eat his friends in the event of an apocalypse, candidates must select which states to focus on for their electoral votes as they plot a path, or several paths, to the White House.

Electoral votes are not to be confused with your common-as-muck votes cast by millions of normal voters at the general election (a.k.a. Election Day on 3 November), though they're obviously connected. The Electoral College is not too dissimilar to a mammoth game of *Play Your Cards Right*. What do points make? Prizes! What do accumulated individual state tallies of electoral votes reaching the required winning total of 270 make? The presidency! I accept it's marginally less catchy. And the 'Brucie Bonus'? Accommodation is thrown in for free, with keys to a very nice house.

Slate Starter

Presidential contenders don't have to get exactly 270 electoral votes to win. That would be silly – though not mathematically impossible.[2] There's a surprising amount going on after Election Day itself for which you can blame the Electoral College. Here's what happens in a bit more detail.

An ordinary voter in an ordinary state (and in D.C. as well) will cast a single vote on 3 November in support of a slate of electors pledged in advance to back a specific presidential-and-vice-presidential ticket. The ballot paper may say something like 'Electors for Trump and Pence' or 'Electors for Biden and Somebody Else' (as of writing, the Democratic running mate is not known). The names of the national candidates will usually be displayed on the ballot (which can be paper or electronic) rather than all the potential electors' names, which will vary in number according to the total electoral votes at stake in the state. Pennsylvania, for example, will have competing slates of 20 electors for both the Democrats and the Republicans as the state has 20 votes in the Electoral College to award, making it an important prize for candidates.

It Doesn't Exist

The chosen electors, each of whom has one electoral vote for president, then meet in their own states. The meetings take place on the first Monday after the second Wednesday in December – presidential hopefuls need stamina, lots of money and a really good day-by-day diary. The 51 separate meetings make up the overall Electoral College. Strictly speaking, the Electoral College is a constitutional device rather than an actual physical institution (as part of my own campaign to explain the Electoral College, I made the decision to break bad news in bits as we go along).[3]

The electors cast their votes and all the tallies from across America are then sent off to be officially accepted and added up in a joint session of Congress in January. The larger the state's population, the more Electoral College votes on offer as a prize to the winner of that individual state contest. California has the biggest prize by far at 55 electoral votes – five times as many as Arizona's 11, or 11 times as many as Civil War baby West Virginia's five. Boring Ohio usually ends up on the same side as the national winner and has 18 electoral votes, twice that of South Carolina's nine votes and six times as many as luscious Vermont on three, which is the lowest number of votes any state can have.[4] Candidates need a finger in several pies, or states, as they seek to build up a winning score. Plenty of pies produce a president's picnic.

Joe *versus* Donald

As well as marking the day of the week when Americans vote on who will become the most powerful adult in the world, *Tuesday's Child* focuses on how the Electoral College decides the winner. 'Tuesday's Child is full of grace' according to the popular nursery rhyme. Donald John Trump was born on 14 June 1946, a Friday. That makes him 'loving and giving' if your chief source of information in a coronavirus-hit election year is nursery rhymes. Joseph Robinette Biden was born on 20 November 1942, also a Friday.

Election Day is the same nationwide under an 1845 federal law which refers to a 'college of electors'.[5] Casting a vote could require a day's travel in an agrarian society to the county seat – America's population was only 23 million in 1850 – and a day's travel back. That ruled out Monday for religious reasons, given that it would have required travel on Sunday, and Wednesday was often market day, which meant Thursday was no better.[6] Handily, November came after harvesting and usually before extreme weather.

Zip forward to the twenty-first century of 330 million Americans and the technology to text votes from the moon (full disclosure: the author has never done this), and Election Day is still Tuesday and the Electoral College remains supreme. It has survived strong criticism from scholars and some politicians through the centuries and has been the subject of hundreds of proposed amendments. 'By most accounts, no other federal institution has witnessed more attempts to amend or abolish it,' wrote Robert M. Alexander, with mention of Gary Bugh's estimate of at least 772 such attempts.[7]

'How did the United States come up with such a crazy way to elect a president?' asked Paul Finkelman, who was obviously not a fan, in 2002. All of 66 years before, the University of Michigan's Joseph E. Kallenbach had contended that 'the abolition of the useless electoral college is a constitutional reform long overdue'.[8] Why are critics so against the Electoral College? Spoiler alert: It might be because winners in the final Electoral College total don't always get more votes nationally from actual voters (the popular vote) than their opponent. If they did, President Hillary Clinton would have been seeking re-election in 2020.

Off to College

The Electoral College's total of 538 is determined by the size of America's Congress. The bicameral legislature has 435 seats in the House of Representatives and 100 in the Senate, two for each of the 50 states. Once you factor in the three electoral votes for Washington, D.C., the Electoral College reaches 538. The Permanent Apportionment Act of 1929 has kept the House of Representatives at 435, apart from temporarily rising when Alaska and Hawaii became states in 1959. This constant number disregards the staggering growth of the U.S. population by more than 200 million since the limit was set.[9]

Democratic stronghold California's 55 Electoral College votes are calculated through adding up its population-based 53 representatives and two senators. Texas is the next biggest with 38 electoral votes – 36 representatives and two senators – followed by New York and Florida with 29 each (27 and two), Pennsylvania and Illinois both on 20 (18 and two) and Ohio with 18. Readers can work this last one out for themselves. Win these seven states and candidates are already on 209 electoral votes and well on their way to 270. In reality, that won't happen. California, New York and Illinois are solid Democratic (blue) states, while Texas has gone Republican for the last 10 elections in a row and Ohio is often red. Florida and Pennsylvania belong among roughly 10 'swing states' in 2020 which could end up blue or red and help determine the overall winner. It's a case of winner-takes-all for most states, with all electoral votes going to whoever gets the most votes in that state. Whether they win by one, 100,000 or 1 million, a candidate gets all that state's votes in the Electoral College – except in Maine and Nebraska, which split them up.

So instead of a straightforward popular vote, with the next president being the candidate who gets the most real votes from real voters across the real nation, the never-to-be-found Electoral College can make it a very different game with huge consequences. Not simples.

Chapter 1, *Donald Duck: Why Trump Ignores California*, looks at how the existence of the Electoral

College fundamentally shapes campaign strategy. Every campaign is a high-stakes presidential pick 'n' mix. Why commit resources to a state where you know you won't get any of its Electoral College votes? Candidates must work out which of the 50 states (D.C. always votes Democrat) to target and win in order to reach that magic number of 270.

Winner Loses Again?

While historically the winner has nearly always won both the popular vote and the Electoral College tally, two of the last five elections have seen the popular vote winner lose the electoral vote.

In 2000, the infamous 'hanging chads' standoff in Florida resulted in George W. Bush beating Bill Clinton's vice president, Al Gore, by 271 to 266 in the Electoral College, with one abstention. It was a rare occasion in modern times where the winner was not clearly known on Election Night, but in the end Gore won the popular vote by around 500,000 more votes than Bush, who famously remarked during the campaign, 'I know the human being and fish can coexist peacefully.'[10]

In 2016, Republican candidate Donald Trump beat Hillary Clinton 304 to 227 in the Electoral College after 'faithless electors' were discounted – we'll get to them – but lopsided victories in California and New York resulted in Clinton getting almost three million more votes nationally than Trump.[11] Huge margins of victory in California and New York produced the anomaly of Trump winning the presidency despite easily losing the popular vote.

This might happen again in 2020 with a different Democratic challenger, Biden, and on an even larger scale. Analyst David Wasserman noted that 'it's possible Trump could win five million fewer votes than his opponent – and still win a second term'.[12] This would mean that three of the last six elections – a whopping 50 per cent – had produced a winning candidate who lost the popular vote, compared to only three – in 1824, 1876 and 1888 – for all the other elections where popular vote records are available.[13] While Trump's campaign would clearly change tactics under a different system where every vote suddenly counted, another minority win in 2020 could put the Electoral College on the constitutional naughty step, perhaps never to return to the democratic classroom.

You're Fired! Maybe

The 2020 showdown was tense even before the trauma of coronavirus, which passed 1,000 deaths in the U.S. on 26 March, 10,000 deaths on 6 April and 100,000 deaths on 27 May.

The 74-year-old Trump is a deeply polarizing and often entertaining candidate who divides his country roughly equally and the world not so roughly equally. But coronavirus deaths have no funny side. It's safe to say that what's been called the 'Lysol Moment', Trump's dangerous suggestion for coronavirus victims to inject themselves with Dettol, did not go down well anywhere, including among those who foolishly followed the president's advice. Trump claimed he was being sarcastic.

Both sides have dished out the insults. Trump called himself a 'very stable genius' in response to opponents' suggestions of mental instability, a charge the Trump camp has also unkindly thrown at Biden. Trump took advantage of nothing less than a prayer breakfast to blast his critics the day after his Ukraine-linked impeachment trial in the Republican-dominated Senate ended in acquittal in February 2020.[14] One of Trump's sons criticized the 77-year-old Biden after he bizarrely called a female student a 'lying, dog-faced pony soldier' at a rally in the New Hampshire primary as he chased the Democratic nomination; he appeared to think he was making a jocular reference to a John Wayne movie. Inheriting his father's shyness on social media, Donald Trump Jr tweeted: 'Are we still pretending that Joe Biden hasn't lost his marbles?'[15]

Age of Coronavirus

Trump starts the campaign with one huge advantage: his last name. Not Trump, but 'Mr President'. Most incumbent presidents win re-election.

However, that was before the world entered the Age of Coronavirus, in which 'Mr President' can suddenly become 'Mr Culpable'. All bets were off ahead of Election Day, with any second wave potentially proving politically disastrous for Trump. It was also before the shocking death of George Floyd on 25 May 2020, which sparked huge protests against police brutality.

Since 1936, only three presidents seeking to stay in office have failed to do so: Gerald Ford in 1976, Jimmy Carter in 1980 and George H. W. Bush in 1992. In the same period, nine sitting presidents in 11 different elections have been returned to the White House, namely Franklin Delano Roosevelt (FDR) in 1936, 1940 and 1944 (before presidents were restricted to two terms), Harry S. Truman in 1948, Dwight Eisenhower in 1956, Lyndon Baines Johnson (LBJ) in 1964, Richard Nixon in 1972, Ronald Reagan in 1984, Bill Clinton in 1996, George W. Bush in 2004 and Barack Obama in 2012.

Nobody can be elected president more than twice since the 22nd Amendment was ratified in 1951. Truman and Johnson originally took office through the deaths of Roosevelt and John F. Kennedy, in 1945 and 1963 respectively; both then won their first presidential elections in 1948 and 1964, and both decided against running again in 1952 and 1968.

In the Beginning

Chapter 2, *How It All Began: The Birth of the Electoral College*, will look at why the Constitutional Convention in 1787 opted for the Electoral College and how it was meant to work.

Remember that voters in the November general election in America are still today not directly choosing a president but selecting a slate of electors (who are often party loyalists) backing a specific candidate. It's early in the book to repeat the point but worth doing so in this case. As the National Archives and Records Administration's Electoral College website puts it: 'When the voters in each State cast votes for the Presidential candidate of their choice they are voting to select their State's electors. The potential electors' names may or may not appear on the ballot below the name of the Presidential candidates, depending on election procedures and ballot formats in each State.'[16]

Individual electors nearly always back the same presidential candidate that voters chose in their state in November. So-called faithless electors – those who abstain or back someone else – have thus far failed to rebel in sufficient numbers to change the outcome of an election; the candidate who effectively secures a majority of pledged electoral votes from normal voters on Election Day has always gone on to be president.

The Founding Fathers, who framed the Constitution after putting their lives on the line to free America from the British Empire, ignored, forgot or underestimated the influence of factions which grew into political parties. No electors from New York took part in the 1789 election due to squabbling in the state legislature, so there were already clues. Once parties were involved in elections, with increasingly bitter battle lines drawn up, the end result was never going to be how the framers originally intended.

It quickly got out of hand. Elections in the nineteenth century were often more brutal than those of modern times, such as the coffin-carrying 1828 campaign which failed to stop Trump's favourite, Andrew Jackson, from coming to power.

He Ain't Heavy, He's My President

Having worked hard to elucidate a strange but arguably effective voting system, Chapter 3, *Mr Tall Goes to Washington*, takes a lengthy but light-hearted detour into that wonderful, wacky world of presidential statistics. It looks at which party has won the most post-Civil War elections, which state has produced the most winners, common years for presidential births, and the average age of first-time presidents. Other questions to be answered: Does the taller candidate usually win? What's the best first name to have? Will the younger candidate win more often than lose?

Chapter 4, *O Ye of Little Fish: Problems with the Electoral College*, examines other objections beside the unhelpfully partisan nature of campaigns to this day and of course the winner not winning. Problems include the previously mentioned faithless electors who don't vote in accordance with Election Day results, and the charge that the whole process can easily become trivialised. This includes the amiable Jimmy Carter, one of the brightest of all presidents, having to come up with a cooking recipe. Other criticism says party-faithful states – big or small – are ignored when their result is in no doubt.

The Electoral College is complex and relatively boring – two powerful factors in keeping it alive for so long. Wander into any bar or café in a non-election year, put gel on your hands, remove your visor and possibly your mask too, sit as far away from the world as possible while not staring in anyone's direction, and you're unlikely to overhear America's voting system as a subject of conversation. The author knows of no bar or pub called 'The Electoral College' where groups of customers have non-constitutionally binding votes on choice of drinks before bar staff make the final decision.

Abolition of the college would create new problems, such as wealthy, independent and unaccountable candidates being able to bypass parties more easily. It could also exacerbate old issues, with smaller states at risk of almost disappearing from campaigns. Even now, psephologists, historians and psychologists agree there's a limit to what anyone will do for three electoral votes in Wyoming.

The First 58

Three chapters take a look at the 58 presidential elections so far, with the occasional titanic contest threatening the nation's unity. The results themselves are often the focus, so apologies in advance for the many major events not mentioned, such as the Seneca Falls Convention in 1848, a landmark event for women's rights. Likewise, Texas-sized apologies for finding time and space to mention which vegetable George H. W. Bush didn't like but not examining the consequences of his son's war in Iraq. It's that kind of book. 'Flipignorant', mixing flippant and ignorant, is the word I think, though my publisher has gone for the more sales-friendly 'conversational'.

Chapter 5, *Father of the Nation to Uncle Abe: 1789–1864*, starts with Independence hero George Washington receiving every single electoral vote for president in both 1789 and 1792 – the only times this has happened in American history. The mood music is soon ruined by the 1800 contest when Thomas Jefferson and his intended vice president, Aaron Burr, the villain in *Hamilton: An American Musical*, accidentally ended up with the same number of electoral votes. That constitutional curveball triggered the Twelfth Amendment, providing separate votes by electors for the president and vice president, which hadn't been the case before then. Modern campaigns start to take shape in 1828 as Andrew Jackson finally powers into office for the Democrats after winning the 1824 popular vote. The first of eight presidents to die in office so far was William Henry Harrison in 1841, not helped by an outrageously long inaugural address in freezing weather.[17] The chapter ends with Abraham Lincoln, widely seen as the greatest president of all time, getting re-elected with the Civil War drawing to a close, before being shot in 1865 at the theatre.

Chapter 6, *The Drinker to the Thinker: 1868–1944*, starts with the formerly hard-drinking Ulysses S. Grant gaining power and includes the 1876 election between Rutherford B. Hayes and Samuel J. Tilden. This remained the gold standard of electoral disputes before 2000, with Hayes winning 185-184, with catastrophic consequences for civil rights.[18] Another 'loser winner' (what I use for the more common 'wrong winner') came in 1888 when

Benjamin Harrison beat Grover Cleveland 233-168. FDR, vanquisher of the Great Depression and the Nazis, rounds off the chapter with an unrepeatable fourth win in 1944.[19]

Chapter 7, *When Harry Met Dewey to Enter the Donald: 1948–2016*, starts with reference to one of the most famous photos in political history. After Truman unexpectedly beat his Republican challenger, Thomas Dewey, the beaming 33rd president held up the *Chicago Daily Tribune* front page bearing the headline 'DEWEY DEFEATS TRUMAN'. The period covers Reagan's 525-13 destruction of Walter Mondale in 1984 with the highest number of votes won by anyone in Electoral College history, and finishes with Trump coming to power.[20]

Election Night

Tuesday's Child calls it a day with *Election Night: By the Dawn's Early Light*, detailing what readers staying up can look out for as early signs of one candidate gaining an edge. It also takes a glimpse at the future.

If Trump wins he will have gone two for two, but ironically his victory would increase the chances of a Democrat winning in 2024. Holding on to power is tricky for a party after the end of a two-termer, as shown in 2000 when Republican George W. Bush was elected after eight years of Bill Clinton, and in 2008 when Obama was elected for the Democrats after Bush's two terms. That potentially opens the door for a speculative but solid bid by New York Representative Alexandria Ocasio-Cortez, who would easily be America's youngest-ever president at 35.

And if Biden wins? Watch out for one heck of a 'victory concession' speech from Trump.

1

Donald Duck: Why Trump Ignores California

Democratic challenger Joe Biden versus Republican incumbent Donald Trump in 2020 may turn out to be the last-ever presidential election between two white men, or white and orange for critics of the president's unusual skin tone.[1]

This chapter looks at how the candidates try to build up an overall score of 270 to win the 538-strong Electoral College. Such calculations invariably include the four biggest rewards on offer – California (55 electoral votes), Texas (38), New York (29) and predictably unpredictable Florida (29). As well as Florida, campaigns target other key 'swing states' like Pennsylvania (20) and Michigan (16) among other double-digit temptations.

After discussing the necessary ingredients for a successful campaign – a united party, a candidate with 'the vision thing' and a balanced presidential/vice presidential ticket – this chapter ends with a look at campaign issues and painful pitfalls in presidential debates. These debates offer White House hopefuls an important last-minute chance to swing undecided voters their way.

The traditional start to campaigning used to be Labor Day in America, the first Monday in September. In an increasingly digital world, however, campaigns have become relentless from the moment the parties have chosen their candidates – sometimes before.

Final Run

The 2020 election looks like being the final run for the White House that will involve two septuagenarians, especially if today's younger voters find themselves facing coronavirus-linked economic challenges for decades to come. Trump will be 74 and Biden 77 by Election Day on 3 November, both doubling the constitutional requirement that presidents must be at least 35 on taking office.[2]

Age brings wisdom, of course. But in a nation always looking forward and forever wanting to believe in a better tomorrow, compare the 2020 race with the 1960 election when 43-year-old John F. Kennedy took on two-term Vice President Richard Nixon, age 47, or with 2000 when George W. Bush (54) and Al Gore (52) faced off.

In 2017, Trump had reached 70 years, 220 days on being sworn in, making him the oldest president for a first term. He appeared heavily favoured to win the 2020 election until the coronavirus pandemic struck and Biden took a clear lead in key states halfway through the year. But that can change very quickly – you just never know.

Some readers may indeed already know the result as coronavirus wreaks havoc with people's lives, the global economy and, less importantly, publishing deadlines.[3] Suddenly, the success of Trump's bid to stay in office will have largely depended on how he is judged to have handled the corrosive course of coronavirus and its brutal cost in American coffins and taxpayer dollars.

Before Trump's shock win in 2016, the *Huffington Post* had given Hillary Clinton a remarkable 98 per cent chance of becoming the next president.[4] Seeking a last laugh in 2020, Trump will once more ignore the elephant in the Electoral College room: California.

California Dreamin'

As well as being disliked by roughly half the population of the United States of America, Trump and Biden have something else in common: they'll both bypass California. Even in his wildest dreams of blending in among the orange groves, Trump knows he can't win any Electoral College votes in California. Biden knows he can't lose any.

The Democrats adore California, where they've won the last seven presidential contests, from 1992 to 2016, after the Republicans reigned from 1968 to 1988. That's 55-0 to Biden before kick-off. California is the biggest prize in the Electoral College, with around a fifth of the 270 required winning total and more than 10 per cent of the 538 votes on offer.

No Republican presidential candidate has won the state since George H. W. Bush in 1988. Since it's a winner-takes-all system – top the popular vote in the state and you get all the electoral votes – there's simply no point in Trump campaigning for the White House in California.

So why spend time discussing California and its political history if the outcome there is so certain? Well, as Republican politicians and voters become more sympathetic to the Electoral College – presumably linked to their party's candidate losing the popular vote nationally in

2000 and 2016 but still ending up the winner – attention shifts to what the Democrats want. A big unknown for any Democrat favouring abolition of the Electoral College and replacing it with a direct popular vote is whether the party would enjoy a net benefit overall. It's a gamble, and nowhere more so than in California.

If every vote was up for grabs, with victory going to whoever got the biggest pile across the whole country, Trump and future Republican candidates would campaign big time in the nation's most populated state – 40-million strong California – and other heavily Democratic states like New York. After his controversial win in 2016, 'Trump was quick to note that if the election were based on the popular vote, he would have campaigned very differently. He maintained that because of the rules of the Electoral College, he ran a campaign to win electoral votes, not popular votes.'[5]

Gold Diggers

Not even Trump has claimed he won California last time out. Hillary Clinton beat Trump in the Golden State by more than 4 million votes – 8,753,792 to 4,483,814. As already noted, the margin of victory or defeat in a state under the existing system is irrelevant. But if the Electoral College was replaced with a single direct popular vote for president, do past elections or patterns in California offer any clues to the state's political future? Put more crudely, how many presidential votes could the Republicans scavenge if they bothered campaigning there?

We've seen that the number of electoral votes for states is determined by the number of congressional seats (Senate and House of Representatives), which is linked to the decennial U.S. Census. The 2020 Census will come too late to affect the 2020 election but will kick in for 2024 and 2028. California has grown to its dominant position from only 13 Electoral College votes in the 1920s, when the Republican trio of Warren Harding, Calvin 'Silent Cal' Coolidge and Herbert Hoover won the state and the presidency in 1920, 1924 and 1928 respectively.

The Democrats won the next five elections in an expanding California, with FDR sweeping up the 22 votes in 1932, 1936 and 1940. FDR won a fourth straight election in 1944 with 25 votes in the Electoral College at stake, and Harry S. Truman won both the state and the White House in 1948. Republican Dwight Eisenhower then clinched California's 32 votes in his two national victories in 1952 and 1956 against the same Democrat, Adlai Stevenson, a widely admired wit who once said he asked one of his sons 'if he had read my last book and he replied "I hope so"'.[6]

California was now tied on 32 with Pennsylvania, behind only New York on 45. Yorba Linda native Nixon won his home state in 1960 but lost nationally and narrowly in the popular vote to Kennedy – that's the official result, anyway – and went on to mount a failed bid for California governor. Always a complex character, Nixon's 1962 gubernatorial loss triggered a memorable news conference where he mixed false smiles with genuine snarls as he told journalists, 'You won't have Nixon to kick around anymore, because, gentlemen, this is my last press conference.'[7]

He's Back

Lyndon Johnson on his Texas ranch did arguably worse things than kick people around (see 1964 election in

Chapter 7). In 1964, LBJ won California for the Democrats in a national landslide. He got 40 electoral votes for his troubles as California closed the gap on New York, now down to 43. Nixon returned and reclaimed California for the Republicans in the turbulent year of 1968, which saw the assassinations of Rev. Martin Luther King Jr at age 39 and Bobby Kennedy, while chasing the Democratic nomination, at 42. Nixon won again in 1972 when California had become the single biggest state in the Electoral College on 45 votes, a top spot it hasn't given up since, and Gerald Ford kept the state for the Republicans in 1976.

Former California Governor Ronald Reagan won the 45 votes at stake in 1980 and 47 votes in 1984. His vice president, George H. W. Bush, won the state in 1988 after spending much of the decade standing behind Reagan in public speeches and nervously trying to figure out the right moment to laugh at the Great Communicator's endless jokes.

California increased its Electoral College score to 54 for Bill Clinton's wins in 1992 and 1996, and the state has stayed Democratic through Gore in 2000, John Kerry in 2004 with today's 55 votes at stake and Barack Obama in 2008 and 2012.

Based on all this, California looks to be in the Democratic camp for the next quarter-century and then some, though a young, charismatic and independent-leaning Republican may fancy his, or far more likely her, chances and opt to chase the forbidden fruit of all those hanging votes. If every vote counted towards the national total, races would get comparatively tighter, with both parties devoting more time and money to the Golden State.

For now, a Democratic candidate must always win this state. California's Electoral College value alone is bigger than neighbours Oregon (7), Nevada (6) and Arizona (11) plus Utah (6), Idaho (4), Montana (3), Wyoming (3), Colorado (9) and New Mexico (5) put together.

If not politically destroyed by the economic consequences of the coronavirus outbreak, Trump's path to power is simpler where the Big Four are concerned: California and New York (29) have long been lost causes for the Republicans. Texas (38) and Florida (29), on the other hand, are most certainly not.

One Star, Many Votes

Texas, the Lone Star State, is the second-biggest reward in the Electoral College, offering 38 votes amid growing Hispanic and Asian American influence. It has risen from only sixth-biggest in 1960, when it had 24 electoral votes.

Trump, promising to build a 'big, beautiful wall' (largely unbuilt) across the country's southern border with Mexico to keep people out, won Texas in 2016 with 4,685,047 votes to Hillary Clinton's 3,877,868. In an example of the faithless elector syndrome, Trump only got 36 of Texas's 38 votes when the state's electors met; one vote went to controversial libertarian Ron Paul, while the other faithless elector backed John Kasich, a Trump rival for the nomination that year who, as Ohio governor, gave a well-meant but badly received impersonation of a Parkinson's sufferer in 2012. (For his part, Trump appeared to deliberately mock a disabled reporter in 2015 but subsequently denied it.) In the vice presidential tally for Texas, running mate Mike Pence came close to copying Trump when he lost one vote to former Hewlett-Packard boss Carly Fiorina. Pence ended up with 305 votes for vice president, one more than Trump's final presidential total.

The Democrats last won Texas in 1976 when southerner Jimmy Carter, a former governor of Georgia, beat Ford. Since then it's been one-way Republican. Reagan took the state in 1980 and 1984, Texas oilman George H. W. Bush won in 1988 and 1992, moody yet witty Bob Dole dominated in 1996, Texas Governor George W. Bush won at home in 2000 and again as president in 2004, John McCain triumphed in 2008, and dog-on-the-car-roof Mitt Romney prevailed the next time round (see 2012 election in Chapter 7).

But the Texans they are a-changin'. A variety of polls 'suggest the Republican stronghold in Texas has weakened over time, reinforcing both experts' and party leaders' beliefs that Texas is up for grabs in the 2020 election cycle', and Trump's insensitive comments on Houston native George Floyd could damage the president's fortunes in the state.[8] Trump is probably still going to win the state in 2020, but if Pence leads the Republican ticket for 2024 he'll have to spend more than a few pounds to chase the 40-plus electoral votes Texas is set to possess.

Follow Florida

Florida gained unwanted worldwide attention in 2000 for its post-Election Day shambles over who it had voted for that year – Gore or George W. Bush, the brother of Florida Governor Jeb Bush, later unkindly called 'Low Energy Jeb' by Trump in the fight for the 2016 nomination. Dubya then won its increased allotment of 27 votes four years later (from 25 in 2000) in a thankfully calmer count.

Obama won the state in 2008 and 2012 before Trump surprised many with what CNN's Wolf Blitzer on Election Night called a 'big, big win for Donald Trump in Florida'. Trump moved ahead of Hillary Clinton 216-197 with

Florida in his corner as a dramatic contest headed towards its finale. Trump ended up with 4,617,886 votes in Florida to Clinton 4,504,975. The next election looks to be another close race, requiring both main parties to rain money on the Sunshine State.

Kristian Ramos, former spokesman for the Congressional Hispanic Caucus, detailed the Democratic dilemma: 'President Donald Trump has done almost everything he can to anger Latino voters. And yet, his support among this crucial portion of the electorate remains surprisingly consistent' from 2016.[9]

The state remains up for grabs.

Blue Apple

Hillary Clinton squashed Big Donald in the state of New York, getting almost 60 per cent of the vote, in a bruising defeat for Trump which ironically shows the potential to improve for Republican presidential candidates if they had any incentive to campaign there. In December 2016, Bill Clinton was poignantly among the 29 who all backed his wife when the state's electors, those chosen by New York's voters to have their say in the overall Electoral College, met in Albany. The 42nd president (1993–2001) said he had 'never cast a vote I was prouder of'. Donald Trump's son, Donald Trump Jr, was a Republican state elector in New York and would have been similarly called upon if his father had won anything, which he hadn't, not a sausage.

Reagan is the last Republican to make New York a red state in his 1984 landslide. The party hadn't been helped in the preceding decade by Gerald Ford initially denying federal help to the financially troubled city of New York in 1975. That action was paraphrased into the famous headline – FORD TO CITY: DROP DEAD – in New York's *Daily News*. Appearing to forget the controversial pardon he gave to his predecessor Nixon, Ford blamed the five words, and one colon, on his narrow 297-240 presidential defeat to Carter the following year.[10] What if Carter had lost New York's 41 electoral votes to his Republican opponent? Do the math(s): President Ford would have won his first presidential election.

Some 42 years after its original classic, the *Daily News* was at it again, this time running with TRUMP TO WORLD: DROP DEAD on 2 June 2017 after the president said the U.S. would be pulling out of the Paris climate accord. A lively subtitle read 'Decides to hell with science, Earth's future'. Three years on, New York Mayor Bill de Blasio wanted federal support in the coronavirus pandemic and tested the headline's value by asking Trump, 'My question is Mr Trump, Mr President: Are you going to save New York City or are you telling New York City to drop dead?'

The Empire State and its Big Apple core love giving Trump and his party in general a Large Raspberry. After Reagan in '84, the Republicans have never looked forward. Michael Dukakis, a governor from neighbouring Massachusetts, won New York against George H. W. Bush in 1988, followed by victories for Bill Clinton (twice), Gore, Kerry, Obama (twice) and Hillary Clinton. It's Trump's birthplace but it's also his political graveyard.

Trump's 'Swingsong'?

Trump, a brutal campaigner at the kindest of times, shocked many pundits in 2016 by demolishing or flipping the 'Blue Wall', which included seemingly perpetual Democratic states in the Northeast and Midwest. The vertical blue ladder of Washington, Oregon and California on the West Coast, however, was immune to the onslaught.

Trump had successfully used widespread anger at the federal government's seeming indifference to problems in the Rust Belt to turn Pennsylvania (20), Michigan (16) and Wisconsin (10) from blue into red states. Trump was the first Republican to win all three of these Great Lakes states in the same election since Reagan in 1984. None of the three had been won by any Republican since Reagan took Pennsylvania and Michigan in 1988, and Wisconsin in 1984. It was a remarkable performance, but repeating it all would be close to miraculous for Trump.

The Donald's election pivoted on attracting support from forgotten workers who feared their lives had been made forever insecure by closed factories and jobs exported abroad. Trump went into the 2020 battle with a mixed record on coal and steel jobs in the industrial Midwest, though a rumoured 1 trillion dollar national infrastructure plan won't have hurt.

If Hillary Clinton had clinched the 46 votes in the three states of Pennsylvania, Michigan and Wisconsin, she would have won 278-260 without deducting the seven faithless electors in other states. As one commentator wrote: 'Donald Trump would not have won this election unless poor and working-class voters in states like Michigan, Pennsylvania, Ohio, North Carolina and Wisconsin had defected from the Democratic Party in favour of his disruptive campaign.'[11]

Pennsylvania, Michigan and Wisconsin will be key to Trump's 'swingsong' as he seeks to go out on a high with a second and final term. They're even more important to Biden, who wants to rebuild a wall – a Blue one – of his own, which would force Trump to seek compensatory states elsewhere.

Pennsylvania's 20 votes were narrowly won by Trump over Clinton – 2,970,733 to 2,926,441 – but Biden will more than fancy his chances here. He was born in Scranton, Pennsylvania, and represented neighbouring Delaware in the U.S. Senate for 36 years, overcoming tragedy right at the start when his first wife, Neilia, and 1-year-old daughter, Naomi, died in a car accident.

Trump took Michigan's 16 votes by less than 11,000 votes. Michigan Governor Gretchen Whitmer has been touted as a possible running mate for Biden and could help take the state away from the president. Whitmer does not like Trump, and Trump does not like Whitmer. But polls suggest Biden is going to win Michigan anyway.

In Wisconsin, Trump won 10 electoral votes by beating Clinton 1,405,284 to 1,382,536. Clinton had bypassed the state during the general election campaign, not helping her cause with the young, both as voters and party workers. Biden will not make the same mistake.

Other States

Clever Ohio has voted like the country as a whole since 1964, and the Buckeye State ended up 'wrong' only twice in the twentieth century – it backed Thomas Dewey in 1944 against national winner FDR and supported Nixon in the very close 1960 contest won by Kennedy. Ohio has kept its record into the twenty-first century, and Trump got its 18 electoral votes with a near half-million majority. He's marginally on course to win Ohio again, though not guaranteed, as it moves from a swing state to Republican.

Illinois has 20 votes to give and Democrats love this seven-time-straight blue state even more than *Joanie loves Chachi* in the *Happy Days* spinoff set in Chicago. Meanwhile, Trump will hope to prevail in Georgia (16 votes) where last time he won by around 200,000 votes. One state he could struggle to keep, however, is North Carolina (15 votes). Trump got 2,362,631 and Hillary Clinton 2,189,316 last time around, but the state is moving towards the Democrats. Coronavirus permitting, the Republican convention – a big glitzy affair where the party's candidate is chosen/crowned and usually gains at least a temporary bounce in the polls – is planned for the state's largest city, Charlotte, in August, which can only help Trump. (It did not permit: see page 163.)

Other double-digit states include 14 votes in New Jersey (a safe seat for the Democrats), and Arizona (held by the Republicans since 1952, apart from being seduced by Bill Clinton in 1996). Arizona's 11 votes could move out of Trump's column and over to Biden's. On the other hand, Trump is daring to dream of winning Minnesota (10 votes), which has been a solid Democratic state for the last 44 years. Washington state, named after the first president when it entered the Union in 1889 as the 42nd state, has been blue since 1988. Hillary Clinton won easily in Frasier Crane's home state last time out but ended up with only eight of the 12 votes – three faithless electors supported former U.S. Secretary of State Colin Powell and one backed Native American activist Faith Spotted Eagle.[12]

Still Here, Still Blue

In our tour of the Electoral College states, spare a thought for Hawaii with its four insignificant votes. It has been strongly Democrat in every election since Reagan took it for the Republicans in 1984. Hawaiians are going to the presidential polls for the first time since a state-wide official emergency alert was wrongly sent out to their phones in January 2018 amid U.S. tensions with North Korea over its nuclear programme. The latter country's supremely confident leader, Kim Jong-un, had only recently warned the United States that 'a nuclear button is always on my desk'. Trump did his best to keep tensions down by replying, 'My Button works!'

Ten days after Trump's retort, a sleepy Saturday morning in Hawaii was rudely interrupted by the state's emergency alert. As Hawaiians enjoying a weekend lie-in reached out for their phones, the 8:07 a.m. alert got straight to the point: 'BALLISTIC MISSILE THREAT INBOUND TO HAWAII. SEEK IMMEDIATE SHELTER. THIS IS NOT A DRILL.' Broadcaster NBC reported that one terrified family in Kailua took shelter in the bathtub. Another message correcting the alert was issued 38 minutes later, though notifications were made before that on Twitter and Facebook assuring citizens that there was no danger. Just to be on the safe side, attention-grabbing signs for busier-than-expected weekend traffic informed drivers, 'MISSILE ALERT IN ERROR THERE IS NO THREAT.' It wasn't yet 9 a.m. The Hawaii Emergency Management Agency official who sent out the alert during a shift change had mistaken a standard missile drill for the real thing. He was later fired.

'The Bernie People'

Can Trump also avoid the sack?

Most tight races, nationally and in individual swing states, come down to a variety of factors. These include turnout, how driven different groups of voters are to stop a particular candidate winning (this could work against Trump in 2020, just as it did against Hillary Clinton in 2016), voters' loyalty to a candidate and party, and, crucially, how independent-minded voters cast their votes.

Prevented by coronavirus fears from holding energy-filled rallies for his predominantly youthful supporters, and trailing badly in the polls anyway, Bernie Sanders announced on 8 April that he was suspending his campaign for the Democratic nomination. The move by the 78-year-old junior senator for Vermont left the way clear for Biden to take on Trump.[13]

While Trump enjoyed stirring the pot by saying 'the Bernie people' should support him instead, Biden went out of his way to praise Sanders. The move was no doubt made with memories of the lingering bad blood from 2016 between democratic socialist Sanders and Hillary Clinton, and more importantly between their supporters, which depressed turnout by significant groups of voters in important states. Hillary Clinton to this day blames Sanders for her defeat. The former New York senator and U.S. Secretary of State claimed 'nobody likes him' when asked about Sanders in Nanette Burstein's Hulu documentary series *Hillary*.

'The Vision Thing'

It seems different this time. Sanders publicly backed Biden at an earlier stage compared to the grudging endorsement he gave Hillary Clinton in 2016. Very wise. Divide a party and you're rarely forgiven. Political life for consumer advocate Ralph Nader was badly damaged after the 2000 election when his third-party candidacy for the

Greens was widely believed by Democrats to have given the presidency to George W. Bush over Gore – Nader got almost 100,000 votes in hotly contested Florida, where Bush won by 537 after intervention by the U.S. Supreme Court.[14] Successful candidates need a united party.

While not appearing desperate, they also have to offer hope, optimism, vigour – think Bill Clinton wearing shades and playing 'Heartbreak Hotel' on the saxophone on *The Arsenio Hall Show* in 1992 – and proudly possess what Bill Clinton's opponent, George H. W. Bush, once awkwardly called 'the vision thing'.

It's nothing new, from FDR convincing America there were better days ahead and a way out of the Great Depression to Bobby Kennedy's last words on earth. Speaking at California's Ambassador Hotel moments before being fatally shot after winning the state's Democratic primary election on 5 June 1968, Kennedy told a packed audience, 'We are a great country, an unselfish country, and a compassionate country and I intend to make that my basis for running.' The national grief, felt more than a half-century on, was for a man who wanted to end the Vietnam War bloodbath and who was overflowing with 'the vision thing'.

Tickets Please!

Biden's vision includes himself as president, a fairer society and a woman as his running mate, making it the fourth time a major party has run with a female on the ticket. Hillary Clinton in 2016 is the only woman so far to head that exclusive ticket. Former prosecutor Geraldine Ferraro was chosen by the Democrats' Walter Mondale as his running mate in 1984. The 44-year-old Sarah Palin became the would-be 'Veep' for 72-year-old Republican John McCain in 2008, helping to balance the ages as well. Both Ferraro and Palin ended up on the losing side but each had a presidential candidate cruising for an Electoral College bruising anyway: a 525-13 annihilation for Mondale against Reagan, and a 365-173 defeat for McCain against Obama.

Balancing Act

Presidential candidates must consider gender and race along with home state and ideological and geographical balances when choosing their running mate. It's nice if No. 1 likes No. 2, and vice versa, but not essential.

After Obama's two-term presidency, gender had until recently topped that ladder of considerations, even more than what the vice presidential pick offered in their own state's electoral votes. Some hopeful candidates can find themselves out of consideration for the job if they come from a state the party knows it will win regardless.

That reasoning doesn't always hold. Current Vice President Mike Pence is a former governor of Indiana (11 votes), which has been Republican since 1968 apart from Obama winning in 2008. Pence had other attributes in favour of his selection. The former talk show host helped to boost the ticket's national appeal to evangelicals and conservatives, and the then 57-year-old also helped on the age issue with voters always wanting to be sure the vice president is ready to take over if the worst happens.

While Trump is hard to define in many ways, ideologically moderate Republican ticket-toppers have regularly looked to conservative hard-hitters to soothe the base. The affable Biden will face a similar dilemma in his pick to avoid disappointing Sanders' progressive and passionate supporters on the left, especially over healthcare and the environment. For age balance alone, even before Biden had committed himself to selecting a woman on his ticket, the choice would not have been Sanders himself, or anyone else in their 70s.

A party's two candidates shouldn't be from the same state (the 12th Amendment says if they are then electors in the same state can't cast their two votes for both of them), but this wouldn't help anyway in the chase for electoral votes. It can make sense to have a geographical mix such as east and west, or north and south, like Massachusetts smoothie JFK and Texan bad boy LBJ in 1960. Against that conventional wisdom, Bill Clinton and Gore succeeded as two young centrist reformers from the South – Arkansas and Tennessee respectively – in 1992, when vision, vigour and a poor economy overcame geographical considerations. Tennessee came back to haunt Gore in 2000 by denying him the presidency after giving its 11 votes to Bush.

Picking Pence

Everyone, not least Pence, is assuming Trump will keep him on the 2020 ticket. The president says, 'He's our man, 100 per cent' so for cynics it's 50-50.[15] Trump has a proven ability to surprise but dumping the vice president – in a typically tactful way on live TV at the party convention with the words 'You're fired!' – would be a major shock even by Trump's impossibly high standards, especially for Pence. Biden could rival that by choosing the enormously popular former First Lady Michelle Obama as his running mate. Don't expect either to happen.

It's getting much less common, but vice presidents do change for a variety of reasons. Gerald Ford's sitting vice president, Nelson Rockefeller, took himself out of consideration for the 1976 election, with Bob Dole chosen to run instead to appease conservatives. Pence fans can relax, however. He will almost certainly stay on and be a strong candidate for the Republican nomination in 2024, with sitting vice presidents usually getting a run for the top spot if they want it.[16]

Black Support

The loyal support of African Americans saved Biden's primary campaign in the 2020 nomination race and he knows it.

Biden could well opt for a black woman as his running mate after riots in the U.S. following the brutal death in Minneapolis of George Floyd, a black man who struggled to breathe while handcuffed and pinned to the ground by law enforcement, including white police officer Derek Chauvin, who had his knee on Floyd's neck for almost eight minutes. In footage of the incident, Floyd repeatedly and clearly says, 'I can't breathe.'

California Senator Kamala Harris and Stacey Abrams, who came very close to winning the Georgia gubernatorial race in 2018 when she would have become America's first black female governor, are among potential Veeps often mentioned. Harris's California is super-safe for Biden anyway, but Georgia, won by Trump in 2016, has a very useful 16 votes at stake. Save for Obama, no African American has been chosen as a presidential or vice presidential candidate by either of the two major parties. No woman has ever served as a vice president. Morally and politically, Biden will be tempted. Stop press. It's Harris.

Election Issues

Expect two timeless issues to feature in the general election campaign: the economy and healthcare, especially in light of the coronavirus pandemic. Racism and the environment may get the attention they deserve in swing states. If the handling of coronavirus itself is the top issue, meaning that voters aren't talking about anything else, that can only be good for Biden.

Things change quickly. At the end of 2019, the U.S. economy appeared in very good shape with record levels of employment and soaring stock markets. Healthcare remained a hugely contentious issue, however, with tens of millions of Americans uninsured before coronavirus sneezed its way on to the scene.

Expect less focus than previously anticipated on the three 'I's – immigration (despite Trump's efforts to raise the issue), the Internal Revenue Service (and Trump's delayed tax returns), and his impeachment on abuse of power and obstruction of justice charges passed in the House of Representatives. Trump was accused of pressuring Ukraine to get information on Biden's son, Hunter, who had worked for a Ukrainian gas company, for use in the 2020 election. The president insisted he had done nothing wrong. Trump survived the resulting Senate trial in 2020, as did Bill Clinton in 1999, and remained president.

America's increasingly tense relationship with China over trade issues and coronavirus has the potential to suddenly move centre-stage, especially if any damaging new detail from China emerges and Trump feels the need to act the strongman. If you're reading this post-election, maybe give a big tick to each correct prediction and forget the wrong ones.

Much of what America has talked about for the last four years won't get much of a hearing, not least the Mueller Report into Russian interference with the 2016 election and any links with the Trump camp, along with possible obstruction of justice by Trump. A rare beast among Trump's critics in being completely unintimidated and strictly non-partisan, former FBI director and ex-Marine Robert Mueller damningly concluded, 'While this report does not conclude that the President committed a crime, it also does not exonerate him.' Trump naturally used this to boast that he had been 'totally exonerated'.

Best Show in Town

One thing's for sure: any campaign featuring Trump and Biden will be highly entertaining and full of verbal 'slips'. Biden regularly gives accidental offence – telling voters 'You ain't black' if they even thought of backing Trump, and saying 10 to 15 per cent of Americans 'are not very good people' – and Trump regularly gives deliberate offence, including his warning during the 2020 riots that 'when the looting starts, the shooting starts'.

From a straight comedic point of view, the 2020 campaign is the best show in town. Biden's 10-15 per cent gaffe was a dangerous reminder to Trump's base of Hillary Clinton's infamous description of half of his supporters as a 'basket of deplorables'. But less than 24 hours later, Trump was back in the headlines after he declared that some unexpectedly good economic forecasts for America represented 'a great day' for George Floyd. You could not make it up. Former Republican National Committee chairman Michael Steele, who is no Trump fan, was scathing on MSNBC's *Andrea Mitchell Reports*: 'I doubt

George Floyd is in Heaven looking down, going "Oh gee, great jobs report!" Are you kidding me?'

Successful campaigns define the issues they want in the spotlight. Bill Clinton's ferocious strategist James Carville, the Ragin' Cajun, stressed 'It's the economy, stupid', at a time when it was in poor shape. Good timing wins many an election. In addition to 'Keep America Great', Trump is trying out 'Transition to Greatness' as a promise to the voters of a marvellous 2021 with the right president in charge. Biden has called himself a 'transition candidate', which is packed with one-term hints of passing the torch to a younger generation of Democratic leaders.

Winning campaigns also seek to tackle any negatives out there. Reagan, in 1981 the oldest president at 69 before 70-year-old Trump took office in 2017, used humour throughout his presidential career in dealing with the age issue. In his first State of the Union address to Congress in January 1982, Reagan quoted America's first president before adding: 'For our friends in the press who place a high premium on accuracy, let me say I did not actually hear George Washington say that.'

TV Debates

Reagan also employed humour to maximum effect when under pressure in presidential debates, which are often the last chance in an election for candidates to really connect with voters – particularly the small tranche of independents yet to make up their minds.

Televised debates between presidential candidates started in 1960 with Kennedy vs Nixon, neither of them president at the time and both with a lot to gain. In the first of four debates, JFK had the chance to show around 60 million of his fellow Americans that there was genuine substance behind this charismatic, great-looking but not terribly hardworking senator. Vice President Nixon had obvious competence but had been advised to lose the 'assassin image' and come across as more of a regular guy to voters; instead he looked 'pale, sweaty, frail, wary', triggering concern from his own mother who, Nixon said, later asked 'if anything was wrong'.[17] At the time Nixon was famously thought to have won the debate on the radio but lost it on TV, though this has subsequently been disputed.

Debates only resumed in 1976 and have kept going through to the present day, with three presidential debates and one vice presidential encounter the typical format. Assuming both candidates turn up, the three presidential debates in 2020 are planned for 29 September in Indiana (11 electoral votes, Trump won in 2016), 15 October in Miami, Florida (29, Trump) and 22 October in Tennessee (11, Trump). The vice presidential debate is on 7 October in Utah (6, Trump).

Oh Yes There Is

Three truly terrible moments for presidential and vice presidential candidates have taken place since 1960. Ford's remarks on the Soviet Union probably affected the eventual result in 1976. Dukakis' perceived weak response over how he would deal with his wife's theoretical violent demise in 1988 cost him votes, but the gentle soul was going to lose anyway (see 1988 election in Chapter 7). Dan Quayle's appalling performance, also in 1988, had little if any impact on that election as his boss, George H. W. Bush, won easily but it remains the most brutal putdown of all time.

Ford's gaffe against Carter came in the second debate on 6 October 1976 at San Francisco's Palace of Fine Arts when the president announced 'there is no Soviet domination of Eastern Europe and there never will be under a Ford administration'. Ford made up considerable ground during the election, but the gaffe may have made all the tiny difference. Ignoring Ford's day job, Carter calmly replied: 'I would like to see Mr. Ford convince the Polish-Americans and the Czech-Americans and the Hungarian-Americans in this country that those countries don't live under the domination and supervision of the Soviet Union behind the Iron – uh – Curtain.'[18]

Get Carter

Carter was less successful when debating Reagan in 1980, a foretaste of 2000 when another knowledgeable, earnest and fact-filled Democrat, Gore, floundered against an easy-going, big-picture-little-detail Republican, George W. Bush. Reagan's best-remembered putdown in dismissing charges from Carter involved a smile, a chuckle, the briefest of pauses and the words, with an actor's fine timing, 'There you go again.'

Biden, no stranger in the past to using other people's lines, may be asking the very same question that Reagan famously asked Americans to consider before voting in 1980: 'I think when you make that decision, it might be well if you would ask yourself, are you better off than you were four years ago?' If the Dems can splash the cash, playing the whole Reagan segment will also reap electoral dividends: 'Is it easier for you to go and buy things in the store than it was four years ago? Is there more or less unemployment in the country than there was four years ago? Is America as respected throughout the world as it was?'[19]

Chasing re-election in 1984, Reagan had a poor first debate against the 56-year-old Walter Mondale before hitting back in their next encounter with a line that made Mondale genuinely laugh: 'I will not make age an issue of this campaign. I am not going to exploit, for political purposes, my opponent's youth and inexperience.'

Quayle Quashed

Dukakis put to death his chances of being elected in the presidential debates against George H. W. Bush, but the same election saw his running mate, Lloyd Bentsen, crush Quayle in the vice presidential debate.

The 41-year-old Quayle defended his youth and inexperience but committed the politically fatal mistake in the debate of comparing his resume to JFK's when the Democratic icon had sought the presidency in 1960. Suspecting that Quayle would make the not entirely outrageous comparison, a riposte had been prepared in advance. Staring at Quayle, who sensibly avoided eye contact, Bentsen delivered this brutal 11-second smackdown which has aged beautifully through the decades: 'Senator, I served with Jack Kennedy, I knew Jack Kennedy, Jack Kennedy was a friend of mine. Senator, you're no Jack Kennedy.'[20]

After the enormous cheers had died down, a wounded Quayle responded, 'That was really uncalled for, senator' and drew some cheers of his own. Too late. He became vice president but his presidential career ended that night.

Jeff's Mate

The knockout blow had an amusing consequence when former president Reagan playfully rebuked Arkansas Governor Bill (middle name Jefferson) Clinton at the 1992 Republican convention. Amid 'We love Ron' signs in the audience, Reagan said, 'Listen to me. This fella they've nominated claims he's the new Thomas Jefferson (jeers). Well, let me tell you something, I knew Thomas Jefferson (cheers). He was a friend of mine (cheers). And, governor, you're no Thomas Jefferson (cheers).'

Come 2000, and Vice President Gore sighed frequently in the first debate against George W. Bush, giving the clear impression he was annoyed at having to debate his inferior. In 2016, the much bigger Trump was widely accused of trying to intimidate Hillary Clinton by wandering around during the debate and lingering behind her as she spoke. His supporters naturally saw it differently. For Nigel Farage, Trump's British buddy and successful Brexit campaigner, the president was 'like a big silverback gorilla prowling the studio'.

2

How It All Began:
The Birth of the Electoral College

As exits go, it was a brave and honourable one.

Just before he was hanged from a tree by the ruling British on 22 September 1776 after an early game of I-Spy, American teacher-turned-soldier Nathan Hale reputedly said, 'I only regret that I have but one life to give for my country.'[1]

Hale died in Manhattan at 21 years old with the American Revolutionary War in full flow. With people like Hale, there was only going to be one eventual winner. The war lasted from 1775 to 1783 and produced more memorable words through the Declaration of Independence in 1776.

The sequence of dates can be confusing as the war was underway in 1775 before the Declaration of Independence. Not as confusing as the War of 1812 (also with the British), which ended in 1815 despite a peace treaty in 1814.

After the good guys won, liberty-loving framers kept a two-faced straight face at the Constitutional Convention in 1787 to define slaves as three-fifths of a human being in the brilliant but conflicted United States Constitution.

And that's where we find the birth of the Electoral College.

By George!

Hot, suspicious, frustrated, distrustful. And make that very hot.

The shorthand version of the Electoral College's origins shows human nature never changes – which, not by chance, was one of the biggest fears of those at the 1787 Constitutional Convention, presided over by George Washington. With the future nation on their shoulders, delegates from a mixed collection of prickly states met in Philadelphia's Independence Hall, originally Pennsylvania State House, from May to September 1787. The stately building had an impeccable resume since it had also produced the Declaration of Independence. Today's visitors get the chance to 'stand in the very room where the United States of America was born'.[2]

The 55 men in attendance at various periods through the summer had bigger issues on their minds than sorting out a procedure to choose a president – everyone thought it was going to be George Washington anyway. Trying to make states work better together, the delegates' main headache was how to balance the rights of big states with those of little states. They left awkward calls on the presidential system to the end, and then agreed on the Electoral College so they could all go home. Big George could take it from there.

Fear Factor

It's obviously far more complicated than that, but the presidency, and specifically the Electoral College, was born out of a deep and wide-ranging suspicion of power and the fear of allowing anyone to dominate, including the bigger individual states and a president with monarchical powers. Americans had given years and lives for the cause, so their concerns were understandable. Even wise and witty Benjamin Franklin took a cautious approach at times, arguing that impeachment needed to be in the Constitution: 'Without impeachment, Franklin urged, the only way to remove an unjust leader was assassination.'[3]

Caution is everywhere in the final document. It was deliberately stipulated that the electors should vote 'for two Persons, of whom one at least shall not be an Inhabitant of the same State with themselves'. This was to encourage a state's electors, initially armed with two presidential votes, to consider other candidates and not just the home-grown one.

Electors were told to meet in their own states rather than one big knees-up with their Electoral College counterparts from around the country with the American people picking up the tab. To be serious, the suspicious eighteenth-century folk behind the Constitution feared smooth-talking and rabble-rousing populists gaining power. Just imagine that happening today! The Founding Fathers wanted to ensure the final choice was taken calmly and responsibly by privileged white male members of society, with white women not getting the vote until the 19th Amendment in 1920. The delegates produced an exciting republican and federal government for an independent America, with a separation of powers, while playing it safe at the same time. The original intention was not to have electors chosen by the people. Indeed, state legislatures selected the electors in early elections.

'The men who gathered in the (Philadelphia) Convention of 1787 were very far from being radical democrats,' wrote Potts. 'In adopting the Electoral College they sought to accomplish two things: First, to avoid the excitement and uproar of popular elections; and, second, to remove the office of President from direct popular control.'[4]

Mr Presidents

Distrust shaped almost everything, such as how long a president should serve. Longer if just one term, say six years, but that could make him all-powerful or a lame duck from the start. Shorter if more than one term but then presidents would seek favour all along to get re-elected. The subject of the president remained a constant but minor niggle for much of the convention.

Or make that *presidents*: 'One vigorous debate surrounded whether the government's executive should be a single person or a board of three.' This problem had a familiar solution: 'Eventually a clear majority voted for a single executive based on the knowledge that Washington would probably be the first President.'[5]

Paine Management

Why everyone thought Washington would be the first president reflected the events which had led up to the Electoral College. Revolution had been a slow burner, despite Britain's foolish George III and insensitive royal representatives in America. The First Continental Congress met in Philadelphia in September 1774 amid anger on the issue of taxation without representation in the British Parliament and in response to Britain's over-the-top Coercive Acts.

Preoccupied Georgia had Native Americans on its mind at the time, so only 12 of the 13 colonies – as shown in the

13 stripes on the American flag – were represented, with little desire by those present to break away from Britain. 'Virtually all of them hoped it was still possible to couple empire with liberty,' one commentator has observed.[6] It wasn't. And maybe it wasn't so amicable after all, since 'both sides, after rubbing each other the wrong way for about 10 years, were spoiling for a fight', according to historian Theodore Draper.[7] The seemingly inevitable happened with the first military clashes at Lexington and Concord in Massachusetts on 19 April 1775, including 'the shot heard round the world'. That most famous of all shots is immortalised in Ralph Waldo Emerson's poem 'Concord Hymn'.

The Second Continental Congress met in Philadelphia in very different circumstances, but still was not ready to declare independence. Future two-term president Washington was appointed commander-in-chief, and the fateful year of 1776 arrived. It looked to be one-way traffic, with 'a loss of faith in all things British, a mood increasingly disposed to favour independence. By January it had found able spokesmen, most notably Thomas Paine in one of the great tracts of the Revolution – *Common Sense*.'[8] The 47-page demolition job by Paine is widely seen as a game-changer, with the English troublemaker declaring that 'even brutes do not devour their young, nor savages make war upon their families' and that 'Europe, and not England, is the parent country of America'. Jolly rude but effective.

Declaration of Independence

Former Vice President and 2020 candidate Joe Biden, or 'Sleepy Joe' to use Trump's term of endearment, was fired up after his 'Super Tuesday' primary successes in March 2020. He was so happy that Biden did what so many politicians have done before him: he quoted the Declaration of Independence.

Biden's impassioned speech included the words 'We hold these truths to be self-evident: that all men and women are created equal'. The veteran Democrat had understandably added 'and women' to the inspiring words penned by slaveholder Thomas Jefferson in the Declaration of Independence.

Underneath the famous date 'July 4, 1776', 10 words at the top of the Declaration adopted by the Second Continental Congress proclaimed 'The unanimous Declaration of the thirteen united States of America'. These united states, sacrificing streams of blood to raise a capital 'U', pledged 'to each other our Lives, our Fortunes and our sacred Honor'.

'Dear John Hancock'

John Hancock's name remains clearly visible on the Declaration of Independence. It was scrawled with precision by the president of the Congress on the original document, which measures 24¼ by 29¾ inches. With Americans often asked for their 'John Hancock', or signature, the various explanations for its size include Hancock simply wanting to wind up the British. According to the National Archives website, Hancock 'used a bold signature centred below the text. In accordance with prevailing custom, the other delegates began to sign at the right below the text, their signatures arranged according to the geographic location of the states they represented. New Hampshire, the northernmost state, began the list, and Georgia, the southernmost, ended it.'

In November 1777, the states agreed the Articles of Confederation, a loose association with each state having one vote. That arrangement was later seen in state delegations in the House of Representatives having one vote each in 'contingent elections' where no president had obtained a majority in the Electoral College. The ineffective Articles would have a major influence on the shape of the future executive. Fully ratified in 1781, they 'carefully safeguarded the states against encroachment from the central government by leaving to them the power of the purse'.[9]

With the war won, and commercial disputes threatening to get out of control, the bickering states knew something had to change.

The Annapolis Accident

The Constitutional Convention came about due to what could be called 'The Annapolis Accident' in September 1786 after influential Virginia pressed for progress between states on trading issues. That low-level meeting in the state of Maryland triggered a full-scale Constitutional Convention the following year in Philadelphia.

Any meeting with Alexander Hamilton present always threatened to take on major significance. In Annapolis, Hamilton and other federalist sympathisers – people looking for a strong national government – seized their chance. 'Those who attended the meeting quickly realized that commerce could not be considered apart from other problems and called for a larger convention in Philadelphia in May of the following year.'[10]

Maryland delegates weren't there, despite Annapolis being the state capital. Despite this, the call from the five states and 12 delegates present gained momentum thanks to Hamilton's impetus. The need for action was shown by Shays' Rebellion in Massachusetts, shifting attitudes among those who had previously been on the fence about further moves.

The Constitutional Convention

And back to the U.S. Constitution. The document finally agreed by delegates in Philadelphia was a multi-layered compromise between big and small states, including the major question over how the national legislature would accommodate both their interests.

That was solved with the Connecticut Compromise, also known as the Great Compromise, with every state having equal representation in the upper-chamber Senate, which would keep an eye on the population-based lower House of Representatives. In a grubby deal – and *puh-leeze*, they knew it was wrong even back then – the Constitution defined slaves ('other Persons') as three-fifths of a human in order to give slave-holding states more seats in the House of Representatives and more influence in choosing presidents.

The inspiration for the Electoral College is often attributed in part to the Holy Roman Empire, where princes were electors for the German king. In more practical terms, however, delegates were simply trying to find a compromise that worked.

Why, Why, Why, Wyoming

When something went right at the convention, delegates remembered it for later. 'The principle of protecting the small states through equality of representation in the Senate was thus extended to the practice of choosing the president in the Electoral College.'[11] Three remains the lowest number of electoral votes for a state, which disproportionately benefits the smaller states compared to bigger ones. The comparison often made today is California being 70 times more populated than Wyoming but having the same number of senators and only around 18 times the number of electoral votes – 55 against three. In the House of Representatives, California has 53 to one.

Fair or unfair, it did the trick.

'The most basic reason that the founders invented the Electoral College was that the Convention was deadlocked on simpler schemes like direct election and choice by Congress, and thus invented a system that could be "sold" in the immediate context of 1787. The chief virtue of the Electoral College was that it replicated other compromises the Constitutional Convention had already made.'[12]

We the People, You the President

The first seven words of the Constitution turned colonies into 'We the People of the United States' with a capital U. But who would lead them? After Washington, that is.

Framers at the convention were often a glass-half-empty lot, wary of other states, but they knew they needed to be practical. The president would be a clear beneficiary since 'the framers had laboured under a weak government from 1774 to 1787, and deliberately rejected that model in favour of stronger central powers. Consciously, at the national level, they vested greater powers in an executive.'[13]

The practical difficulties for electing a president were obvious to anyone who had travelled to the convention. After James Madison, 'General Washington arrived second, having taken five days to cover the 140 miles (225 kilometres) from Mount Vernon in his own carriage, driven by his slaves'.[14] That journey alone helps explain that arranging a presidential election with a simple direct vote on the same day was a non-starter. Even making the candidates known wasn't easy.

'How should the president and vice president be elected? That was one of the most difficult issues the convention faced,' Maier wrote. 'Some delegates thought the people should elect them – but would the people have sufficient information about candidates from distant parts of the country? That seemed so doubtful that the task was entrusted to an idiosyncratic "electoral college", whose structure and procedures were described in detail (Article II, Section 1, paragraph 3).'[15] It was a paragraph which would need fixing less than 15 years later, with a top-two twist in the tale for the 1800 election.

The Small Print

Sections 1 to 4 of Article II provide plenty of detail, including eligibility for the presidency. The Constitution says a president must be at least 35, a natural-born U.S. citizen (taken to include potential presidents like John McCain, born in the Panama Canal Zone) and a resident for 14 years. Although the Constitution doesn't specifically say you can't run in your 20s, it would be a waste of everyone's time with early intervention or any votes just not counted.

One part says you qualify if you were 'a Citizen of the United States, at the time of the Adoption of this Constitution'. No longer of use to anyone, the 'provision was added to satisfy delegates such as Pennsylvania's James Wilson, an immigrant from Scotland, who objected to being excluded from high office by a constitution he had helped write'.[16]

Joe Publius

Worried it might be forced to stump up some hard 'cash' for its paper debts, Rhode Island had missed the Constitutional Convention altogether. Although it was the first colony to declare independence, Rhode Island was the last of the 13 states to ratify the Constitution, 34-32, in 1790. The order in which the 13 states ratified the Constitution is the same number at which they joined the Union. 'The First State', Delaware, is forever on top, with Pennsylvania second and New York 11th.

The intellectual battle in New York left behind a famous series of essays, which we now know as *The Federalist Papers*, published in newspapers by authors like Hamilton and James Madison to persuade the key state to ratify the new Constitution. Then, as now, New Yorkers liked to be convinced.

Always keen to stress the differences between the proposed future president and the current British monarch, Hamilton wrote in No. 69 under the pseudonym Publius that 'the President of the United States would be an officer elected by the people for *four* years; the king of Great Britain is a perpetual and *hereditary* prince'. Hamilton gets boastful in the key essay, No. 68, defending the Electoral

College, saying, 'If the manner of it be not perfect, it is at least excellent.' In the same essay, Hamilton assured readers there was little danger of the country electing an unqualified rabble-rouser:

> Talents for low intrigue, and the little arts of popularity, may alone suffice to elevate a man to the first honors in a single State; but it will require other talents, and a different kind of merit, to establish him in the esteem and confidence of the whole Union, or of so considerable a portion of it as would be necessary to make him a successful candidate for the distinguished office of President of the United States.[17]

Count to 12

It wasn't as excellent as Hamilton thought. Electors had been given two votes each, with the top two candidates becoming president and vice president respectively. That was all well and good when someone got the most votes, but what happened if an intended president and vice president from the same party accidently ended up in a tie for the top job?

Amid the unexpected rise of parties, America was about to find out in 1800 when Thomas Jefferson and his assumed vice president, Aaron Burr, got the same number of votes. Cue constitutional discombobulation and major surgery as early as 1804 when the 12th Amendment spared everyone's blushes. The situation had not been helped by Burr realising that he actually wouldn't mind being president. As laid out in the Constitution, the first contingent election where the result was determined by the House of Representatives (see 1800 election in Chapter 5) finally ended when Jefferson prevailed on the 36th ballot.

The 12th Amendment, ratified in 1804, really spells it out to make sure there's no ambiguity or misunderstanding. Electors 'shall name in their ballots the person voted for as President, and in distinct ballots the person voted for as Vice-President'. Ordinary voters cast the one vote for the presidential-vice presidential ticket, e.g. Trump-Pence, but electors could cast one presidential vote for Pence and one vice presidential vote for Trump, possibly depending on state laws on faithless voters. In addition, the 12th Amendment kept the voting restriction on home state candidates, specifying that either the presidential or vice presidential candidate 'shall not be an inhabitant of the same state' as electors.

Here's a fanciful example. Trump could dump Pence and sensationally select prominent critic Robert De Niro as his running mate. That's not going to happen, but if it did both the president and vice president picks would be from New York (although Trump is now based in Florida, so it's a poor example). Ignoring that Floridian fact, this means that the New York presidential electors chosen by voters on Election Day (who are not going to end up Republican anyway, so this example is raging bull) could not then give their votes to both Trump and De Niro. The electors would have to choose between the two. Between you and me, I think they would choose De Niro.

The choice of president was once again back in the hands of the House of Representatives 20 years later (see 1824 election in Chapter 5) for what has so far turned out to be the last presidential contingent election. It was thought by some delegates in Philadelphia that contingent elections would become the norm, giving smaller states important parity with the bigger states under the one-vote-one-state rule. That hasn't happened.

20th Amendment

The Bill of Rights – the first 10 Amendments – quickly followed on from the Constitution.

A law in 1845 set the first Tuesday after the first Monday in November as Election Day for all states, possibly with the intention of avoiding All Saints' Day on 1 November. The move was inevitable in the long run as communications got faster and results needed to come in around the same time, or you would risk results affecting votes. This danger stretched as far into the future as 1980 when Carter upset many in his party by conceding to Reagan before voting had ended on the West Coast. It's not known whether Carter offered critics a prime-time slot on the White House tennis court as a peace gesture (see start of Chapter 4).

The 20th Amendment, ratified in 1933, shortened the gap between the presidential election and when the winner would be sworn in. It applied from the 1936 election, meaning that FDR took the oath under the old system on 4 March 1933 – a gap of four months since winning the 1932 election at a time of economic crisis, leaving President Herbert Hoover ineffectively dealing with the Great Depression. After FDR won the 1936 election, however, he was sworn in on 20 January 1937, which remains the same today.

22nd Amendment

The 22nd Amendment brought in two-term limits by declaring that 'no person shall be elected to the office of the President more than twice'. It was seen as a response by the Republicans to FDR's mammoth tenure from

1933 to 1945, with four election wins. As it was ratified in 1951, Harry S. Truman – see what the 'S' stands for in next section – wasn't affected by the 22nd Amendment but chose not to run again. Future vice presidents who become president can't chase a second election win if they originally came to power with more than half a term left.

Ironically, Truman's successor Dwight Eisenhower was affected by the change and didn't have the option of running again in 1960.

25th Amendment

Truman lacked two things in life: a middle name and a vice president. The Harry S. Truman Presidential Library & Museum has the president explaining 'that the "S" did not stand for any name but was a compromise between the names of his grandfathers, Anderson Shipp Truman and Solomon Young'.

One consequence of Truman assuming the presidency in 1945 after FDR's death was that he would have no vice president. There was no replacement procedure in place, and Truman had to wait until his surprise 1948 election win when Alben W. Barkley was elected vice president. We have one word to thank Barkley for: 'Veep'. According to the official senate.gov website, 'His young grandson had suggested this abbreviated alternative to the cumbersome "Mr Vice President". When Barkley told the story at a press conference, the newspapers printed it, and the title stuck.'

LBJ was also without a vice president when he became president following JFK's assassination. After the 25th Amendment was ratified in 1967, no president would ever be without a vice president again. The president nominates a vice president who must be confirmed by a majority vote in both the House of Representatives and Senate. Gerald Ford became the first man to gain the No. 2 slot this way in December 1973 (after Spiro Agnew resigned over tax evasion and a bit more than that) and could send Christmas cards as Vice President that year. The following year those cards were from the president, still unelected.

The same 25th Amendment also lays out what happens when the president is unable to perform his duties and is replaced by the vice president.

Tidy Time

To this day electors gather in their own states to sign their certificate of votes, with varying degrees of neatness. North Carolina's certificate of 15 votes for Trump in 2016 appears very smart, with signatures above typed-out names and their district. The signatures page on Illinois' 20 votes for Chicago-born Hillary Clinton is nowhere near 'night on the lash' level but could be tidied up a tad for 2020.

Then it's waiting for the official vote tallies of all the December meetings to make their way to Washington, D.C., and be opened and counted in a joint session of Congress on Wednesday 6 January 2021, assuming no arguments at this stage over their validity.

That leaves only one hurdle for the incoming president: taking the oath on Wednesday 20 January. It's not a time to relax.

Oathmeal

The 35-word Oath of Office is in the Constitution and all presidents since Washington have taken it before becoming president. Only Franklin Pierce (1853–57) has chosen to 'affirm' rather than 'swear' to 'preserve, protect and defend the Constitution of the United States'.

The Supreme Court has never been asked to rule on punishment for verbally mangling the oath. That's just as well since two of the country's brightest men – incoming President Barack Obama and Supreme Court Chief Justice John Roberts – famously messed up the recital in 2009 in front of well over a million people and a global TV audience. The historic occasion for America's first black president rightly took all the headlines but the oath-taking ceremony went so catastrophically awry that the not so dynamic duo was forced into a drastic remedy.

Take One stumbles close to the start as Roberts and Obama accidentally speak at the same time, and it quickly gets worse with First Lady Michelle Obama possibly stifling a smile. The chief justice, seen by fans and critics alike as intellectually brilliant, appears to have memorised the oath. That may have been the problem. In shades of the Morecambe and Wise 'Andre Preview' comedy sketch, Roberts uses the right word, 'faithfully', but in the wrong place. Obama then momentarily improvises. Amid worries the slipup could invalidate the ceremony, and potentially Obama's presidency in a golden era for conspiracy theorists, the pair had to repeat the recital the following day in the White House.

The incident also raises the possibility that 2020 could see an unusual battle for office between two men who have both already been president after media speculation that Obama's vice president, Biden, had actually led the nation for a day after the oath kerfuffle. Ben Macintyre wrote in

The Times, 'Whatever the reason (for the oath wobble), according to some constitutional theorists Mr. Obama did not become President, which made his deputy Joe Biden, albeit briefly, the president.' However, assurances were made that 'Mr. Biden did not take advantage of this sudden honour.'[18]

The potential crisis was all resolved by Obama taking the oath for a second time. In a sign of his governing style to come, 'No Drama' Obama semi-joked to Roberts ahead of Take Two: 'We're going to do it very slowly.'

After Obama was re-elected, the 2013 ceremony went ahead smoothly with the Chief Justice appearing to read the oath in a public ceremony on Monday after a private ceremony on Sunday 20 January. The cheeky media observed that Obama had now joined the exclusive 'four oaths club', with FDR being the only other member.

The Story Continues

The Declaration of Independence in 1776 would eventually lead to freedom from the British Empire. The 1789 Constitution put the structure of that freedom in writing and introduced the American people to the Electoral College. For some, removing the Electoral College is the final democratic step to be taken. Others have praise for the hidden wisdom of the Constitution. 'In the day-to-day turmoil of living out the Constitution, Americans came to see that it had set up a President to keep an eye on Congress, and a Congress to keep an eye on the President, and a Supreme Court to keep an eye on both of them,' wrote veteran U.S. observer Alistair Cooke, whose body would quite literally be snatched for spare parts after his death at 95 in 2004.[19]

For now, the jury was definitely out: 'Would it work? No one knew for certain at the start and, in fact, apart from accepting that George Washington would be the first president, no one knew exactly what would happen next. What a story it is!'[20]

3

Mr Tall Goes to Washington

Statistics, like life, can change in significance as the years go by. There used to be a '20-year curse' in American history, with all presidents elected in the 1840, 1860, 1880, 1900, 1920, 1940 and 1960 elections going on to die in office, often violently. Windbag William Henry Harrison died in 1841, Abraham Lincoln won a second term but was assassinated in 1865, James Garfield was shot in 1881, William McKinley was already a second-termer when assassinated in 1901, Warren Harding died in 1923, Franklin Delano Roosevelt (FDR) died in office in 1945, and John F. Kennedy (JFK) went to Texas in 1963.

Politicians still naturally chased power in those election years. Ronald Reagan ended any lingering concerns by surviving John Hinckley Jr's assassination attempt in 1981 and serving out two terms. George W. Bush, elected in 2000, did likewise and without being shot. But it's one to remember.

This chapter looks at four main areas: 1) Presidential statistics, including biggest Electoral College wins, largest popular votes and which party has won the most elections; 2) Presidential names: Does a shorter surname beat a longer one? What happens when equal-letter candidates like Biden and Trump face each other? What's the most common presidential first name? 3) Presidential ages: Does young beat old in a campaign? Who are the youngest and oldest presidents? What's the biggest age transition from one president to the next? And 4) Presidential trivia, including height, hair, sight and star signs. The chapter finishes with a light-hearted look at links between election outcomes and major world events like the Eurovision Song Contest, with some presidential animal wordplay thrown in as a treat for readers.

Do Mention the War

Boring bits first. The biggest wins don't count George Washington's unanimous votes of 69 and 132 in 1789 and 1792, and James Monroe's essentially unopposed 231-1 victory in 1820. Unless otherwise stated, statistics refer to presidents on first taking power, i.e. Inauguration Day for their first term in office or when unelected presidents are sworn in.

The first post-Civil War election of 1868 is often used as a starting point of reference since every race since then to the present day has been between Democratic and Republican candidates, though 1912 was a genuine three-way contest. Some statistics are from post-Second World War elections only.

First and last names used are the ones presidents are known by, not always their original or formal names. It's Gerald Ford, not Leslie Lynch King Jr, Bill Clinton not William Jefferson Blythe III, and Dwight D. Eisenhower, not David D. Eisenhower.[1]

Winners are those who became president, not necessarily those who won the popular vote.

The endless data forms a gigantic statistical puzzle but it won't reveal the simple stark characteristic of presidential winners staring every voter in the face: they really want to win.

Presidential Statistics

500 and Over Club

Winning candidates have reached 500 or more Electoral College votes in only three of the 27 elections since 1912 with at least 531 electoral votes on offer. No election before 1912 had more than 483 votes.

The biggest electoral thrashing came in 1984. Reagan won 525-13, with Walter Mondale securing only his home state of Minnesota and Washington, D.C.

In 1936, FDR beat Alf Landon 523-8 with the unfortunate Democrat winning only Maine and Vermont. This is the all-time biggest win for contested elections in terms of Electoral College vote percentages. FDR got 98.49 per cent or 523 out of 531, compared to Reagan's 97.58 per cent or 525 out of 538.

In 1972, Richard Nixon whacked George McGovern 520-17 (96.65 per cent) with only Massachusetts and D.C. holding out. It could have been 521 but philosopher John Hospers won one vote for the Libertarian Party from a faithless Virginia elector in the presidential tally. So did Hospers' running mate, radio/TV producer Theodora 'Tonie' Nathan, for the vice presidency in what was the first vote for any woman in the Electoral College. David Boaz additionally noted that 'Nathan was also the first Jewish person to receive an electoral vote'.[2]

50 and Under Club

Most candidates can only dream of joining the 500 Club. Some would have settled for simply reaching triple figures.

The worst showing by a Republican Party candidate since 1868 is a tie between challenger Alf Landon with his eight electoral votes in 1936 and William H. Taft, also with eight (Utah and Vermont), in 1912. Taft's showing is particularly appalling since he was a sitting president. As well as fighting Democratic opponent Woodrow 'Rather Racist' Wilson, Taft faced a formidable third-party challenge from former Republican President Theodore (Teddy) Roosevelt, who won 88 electoral votes. Taft got the lowest electoral vote by any incumbent president, but, uniquely for a president, would go on to hold his dream job as Supreme Court Chief Justice (1921–30). Jimmy Carter is the next-lowest White House incumbent on 49 votes in 1980.

The worst showings by a Democratic Party candidate since 1868 are Mondale, who went out with 13 electoral votes in 1984, and Horace Greeley, who went out with a bang and no votes whatsoever in 1872. Greeley, a newspaper editor and anti-slavery campaigner, really doesn't belong in the loser list. He was a breakaway Liberal Republican fusspot also supported by the Democrats.[3] In a challenging fourth quarter, Greeley's wife died on 29 October. A heartbroken Greeley lost the election on 5 November, and himself died on 29 November. In the end, 63 electoral votes secured by Greeley would eventually be spread out to others. One to re-read on a bad day.

Master of Electoral College

FDR mastered the Electoral College like nobody before or since with a huge overall total of 1,876 votes from four elections – 472 (1932), 523 (1936), 449 (1940) and 432 (1944). Shame it wasn't 1,776. He had the votes to spare. Reagan, despite the two-term limit now applying, is the other president to have reached triple figures (1,014), and his electoral vote average is higher than FDR's after wins of 489 (1980) and 525 (1984). Eisenhower is third overall on 899 with 442 (1952) and 457 (1956). Nixon also qualifies for the champions league in fourth spot on 821 with 301 (1968) and 520 (1972).

The lower two-term totals for more recent presidents like George W. Bush (557), Bill Clinton (749) and Barack Obama (697) possibly show the effect of increased partisanship where voters are less inclined to vote for presidents not from their usual party.

Grover Cleveland is the only candidate apart from Roosevelt to top the popular vote three times, winning in 1884 (219), losing in 1888 (168) and winning in 1892 (277) for a combined total of 664 electoral votes. Nixon may have won the 1960 popular vote though not the presidency itself (under a proposed re-examination of Kennedy's total) to go with his two wins in 1968 and 1972.

Win 49, Lose 1
Former California Governor Reagan and former would-be California governor Nixon have another special bond: they're the only two presidents to win 49 of 50 states (98 per cent) or, to be mean, 49 out of 51 contests (96.08 per cent) including Washington, D.C. FDR won 46 of 48 (95.83 per cent) in 1936 with Alaska and Hawaii not having gained statehood and D.C. not yet in the electoral mix.

Nixon was unable to exploit his landslide as much as he would have liked, swearing (in) once again in January 1973 and resigning in August 1974 over the Watergate scandal. A rough glance at the map indicates 'Tricky Dicky' won more square metres of American soil than any other candidate – the only state he lost in 1972, Massachusetts, being smaller than Minnesota in 1984 and Maine and Vermont combined in 1936.

Nixon remains the president with the all-time biggest margin of victory at 18 million votes – 47,169,911 to McGovern's 29,170,383. In that sense only, as Nixon was never truly loved in his entire career, America's most popular president remains the only one to have resigned.

Reagan won the popular vote in 1984 by around 17 million and LBJ in 1964 by 16 million.

Pop-ups
Nixon won in 1972 with 60.7 per cent of the vote but that fell just short of the biggest popular vote percentage. This is held by Lyndon Johnson with 61.1 per cent in 1964 when he romped home 486-52 against Barry Goldwater. FDR got 60.8 per cent in the 1936 election.

Comparing actual number of votes rather than percentages is unfair since the population has grown considerably over the years.

Let's do it anyway.

The top three are all Democrats, all in the 21st century, but not all are presidents. Barack Obama, like Bill Clinton a formidable campaigner, leads with just under 69.5 million votes in 2008 and 65.9 million in 2012. A non-president comes third. Hillary Clinton recorded a 'losing' score of 65.8 million in 2016. It's a common observation, but, apart from Obama (twice), Hillary Clinton got more votes for president than anyone else in the history of the United States, including her opponent Trump and her husband Bill Clinton. In his defence, President Clinton could tell presidential candidate Clinton that 33 million more Americans voted in 2016 than 1992.

What makes Hillary Clinton's total even more impressive is that she was a deeply unpopular candidate in sections of her own party and country, and waged an over-confident campaign which received a horrible late shock courtesy of the FBI (see 2016 election in Chapter 7).

Party Time

For LBJ, the No. 1 rule in politics was 'Learn to count'. From cajoling as Senate majority leader in the 1950s to barking out orders from the ranch crapper in the 1960s, LBJ knew what needed to be done and whose support he needed to get legislation passed.

For parties busy doing endless Electoral College calculations, the recent past is no comfort. Before Trump came to power, party winners from 1984 to 2012 had been a symmetrical R-R-D-D-R-R-D-D or Reagan-Bush Sr-Clinton-Clinton-Bush Jr-Bush Jr-Obama-Obama.

The three closest Republican-Democrat electoral vote outcomes are: Rutherford B. Hayes beat Samuel J. Tilden 185-184 in 1876; George W. Bush beat Al Gore 271-266 in 2000; and Wilson beat Charles Evans Hughes 277-254 in 1916. Wilson, the only Democratic winner in these three races, was a spoilsport by winning the popular vote as well.

For the 152 years from Ulysses S. Grant's presidency in 1869 to Trump's or Biden's Inauguration Day in 2021, the Republicans will have been in power for 88 years, helped by being the winning Civil War party, and the Democrats for 64 years. The Republicans have won 22 of the 38 elections from 1868 to 2016, and the Democrats 16.

The Republicans dominated after the Civil War and earned the GOP (Grand Old Party) tag for keeping the country together, an historic achievement appreciated even more now in a non-partisan way as America again tries to come to terms with its past. The Republicans won in 1868, 1872, 1876, 1880, 1888, 1896, 1900, 1904, 1908, 1920, 1924, 1928, 1952, 1956, 1968, 1972, 1980, 1984, 1988, 2000, 2004 and 2016.

In 1884, Grover Cleveland was the first Democrat to win a presidential election since James Buchanan in 1856. Wilson exploited a split opposition to win in 1912 and end 16 years of Republican rule. The Democrats later enjoyed 20 years in office, from 1933 to 1953, through four-time winner FDR and Harry Truman. Bill Clinton halted three straight Democratic losses with victory in 1992. The Democrats won post-Civil War in 1884, 1892, 1912, 1916, 1932, 1936, 1940, 1944, 1948, 1960, 1964, 1976, 1992, 1996, 2008 and 2012.

Pick a Number
Those are the years, how about the days? Is there a particular 'First Tuesday after first Monday in November' number where one party does better than the other?

The usual pattern of November election days is 3-5-7-2-4-6-8, with the 2024 election on 5 November and the 2028 showdown on 7 November.

Republicans have won the most elections on four of the possible seven Election Days between 2 and 8 November since 1868. They're ahead 3-2 on 2 November, 4-2 on 4 November, 5-1 on 6 November (pity the Democrat running in 2040) and 3-2 on 7 November. Successful Democratic candidates lead 3-2 for elections on 5 and 8 November.

Ahead of the 2020 encounter, America has held six previous elections on Tuesday 3 November since the uniform date was set in 1845 – it's a 3-3 draw.

'Recent' form favours the Democratic Party with a comfortable win for Bill Clinton in 1992 and landslides for LBJ in 1964 and FDR in 1936. The previous trio of 3 November elections were won by Republicans: all-time heaviest president Taft in 1908; McKinley in 1896; and Civil War hero Grant in 1868.

By the way, Washington is one of only four presidents sworn in during T. S. Eliot's 'cruellest month' of April. The other three – John Tyler, Andrew Johnson and Harry Truman – were vice presidents elevated after the deaths of William Henry Harrison, Lincoln and FDR respectively.

Our Guy

Two states stand out for providing presidents in bulk – Virginia and Ohio. Kentucky has only had one president, but it was Lincoln, who made his political career in Illinois.[4]

Eight presidents have come from Virginia. The state dominated the early years of the nation and its presidency, with four of the first five leaders and seven of the first 12. Apart from William Henry Harrison, his rapid successor John Tyler (1841–45) and Zachary Taylor (1849-50), the Virginians make a significant group of presidents: George Washington, Thomas Jefferson, James Madison, James Monroe and Woodrow Wilson, who is remarkably the last Old Dominion president to hold office from 1913 to 1921.

Ohio is the second most successful state with seven presidents, all from 1869 to 1923, but generally having a far worse fate than Virginia's chosen ones. The first to get hugs from the American people was Grant, born Hiram Ulysses Grant. He's the only president from the Buckeye State to have served a full second term, albeit a terrible one. To be fair, three of the seven died in office, including the assassinated Garfield and McKinley, plus Harding who perished while president in 1923. Hayes, Benjamin Harrison and Taft were also Ohio natives. Virginian William Henry Harrison was a former Ohio senator to give the state a claim to a 50 per cent incumbent death rate.

New York state has provided America with five presidents, namely the two Roosevelts, Martin Van Buren, Millard Fillmore and Queens, New York-born Trump.

Democratic stronghold California's ironic influence on the modern-day Republican Party is shown by its single native president, Nixon – 'Welcome to California, birthplace of Richard Nixon' has not yet taken off – and Illinois-born Reagan. No California governor before or since Reagan's 1967–75 spell in Sacramento has gone on to the presidency. California Governor Pete Wilson was tipped to end this surprisingly sparse record when the former Marine chased the 1996 Republican nomination to take on President Bill Clinton. Wilson was an election-winning machine. He had been elected and re-elected as mayor of San Diego, elected and re-elected as U.S. Senator for California, elected and re-elected as governor of California. White House chases are something else altogether, however, and Bob Dole won the 1996 nomination.[5]

Former Delaware senator Biden was born in Scranton, Pennsylvania, and would be the only native president from that state apart from Buchanan.

Presidential Names

Two's Company
No last name has been shared by more than two presidents.

We have distant cousins Teddy Roosevelt and FDR; father-and-son one-term specialists John Adams and John Quincy Adams; another father-and-son combo in George H. W. Bush and George W. Bush; and grandfather William Henry Harrison and grandson Benjamin Harrison, who gave a shorter inaugural address (but still pretty long) and ended up a one-term president as well. Andrew Johnson and LBJ are unrelated.

Five-a-side

Buchanan (1857–61), criticized then and now for his failure to stop America moving closer to Civil War, did at least have eight letters to his name. Indeed, candidates with longer names won 20 elections from 1868 to 2016, with 15 victories for the short brigade and three elections involving candidates with names of the same length. But 'shorties' remain unbeaten in the last four elections where they came up against a candidate with a longer surname – George W. Bush vs John Kerry, Obama vs John McCain, Obama (and Seamus) vs Mitt Romney, Trump vs Hillary Clinton.

Both Trump and Biden are five-letter surnames in what will be America's first Democratic–Republican game of presidential five-a-side. That psephological nugget could impress at the other kind of party. Before this, the 20th and 21st centuries have seen only three equal-letter contests and two of them were extremely close. George W. Bush beat fellow-four Gore in 2000, Reagan easily defeated Carter in the six-letter club in 1980 and Wilson went to bed at sixes and sixes on a chaotic Election Night in 1916 thinking he had probably lost against Hughes. He hadn't.

The most common surname length for winners is six letters, with nine presidents. The shortest last-name presidents are the four-letter quintet of James Polk, Taft, Ford, Bush and Bush. Only once since 1868 has a major party put up a three-letter candidate, when the Democrat James Cox, Governor of Ohio, lost 404-127 to his seven-letter nemesis Harding in the 1920 election. The Democratic vice presidential candidate in that election had the last laugh, however, a certain FDR going on to win a record four presidential races.

Both Roosevelts fell one letter short of the record 10-letter Washington and Eisenhower. One small addition by Democratic candidate Adlai Stevenson would have made it an equal-letter contest in 1952 and 1956, but all indications are that Eisenhower would still have given 'Stephenson' a rocket.

Eisenhower, often known by his much shorter nickname Ike, remains the only president with five vowels in his surname.

Not There Yet

We're yet to see an actual Mr Smith go to the White House, despite Al Smith's attempt in 1928, which opened the way for fellow Catholic JFK in 1960. Stevenson also failed for the 'S' brigade. Other presidential surname initials remaining unrepresented after 230 years are I, Q, U, X, Y, Z.

Most common first name for a president is James, with five – Madison, Monroe, Polk, Buchanan and Garfield – but James the Last was elected in 1880, with Garfield shot in 1881. It's six and last elected in 1976 if you count Jimmy Carter (born James Earl Carter). John has four presidents, or five with Calvin Coolidge's actual first name. George and William, not counting Bill Clinton, have three.

One-off first names include Herbert (Hoover), Dwight (Eisenhower) and Donald (have a guess). David Dwight Eisenhower 'was named after his father but from childhood was called by his middle name to avoid confusion between the two'.[6] Grover stands alone, though the president was born Stephen Grover Cleveland. Woodrow Wilson had doubts about his first name, Thomas, and dropped it.

The 1996 Republican candidate proudly pointed out that America had 'never had a president named Bob'. Adding 'Bill Beats Bob' to a list of golden rules to remember when campaigning, Bob Dole lost to Bill Clinton.

Presidential Ages

Does Age Matter?

In 38 White House elections since 1868, the older candidate has won 20 times and the younger one 18. Older Republicans – which Trump is not – and younger Democrats – which Biden is not – have a better chance of winning based on past results.

Remember that Trump was older than Hillary Clinton in 2016 but is younger than Biden in 2020. An older Republican contender has won 14 times and younger Republicans have won eight. An older Democratic candidate has won six times and younger Democrats 10.

Nobody so far born in the 1810s (too late), 1930s (seriously pushing it) or 1950s (get a move on) has become president. The 1960s-born Obama jumped the 1950s and the 2020 election has gone back to the 1940s with 1942-born Biden and 1946-born Trump.

Two decades stand out by producing four presidents: the 1800s, including Lincoln (1809), and 1910s, including Reagan (1911) and JFK (1917). The most common year of birth for a president is 1946, which produced a modern-day trio of presidents in Bill Clinton, George W. Bush and Trump.

Youngest and Oldest

The average age of a first-time president is 55-and-a-half years. At 43 years, 236 days on Inauguration Day, Kennedy

(1961–63) remains the youngest elected president and the youngest president to die in office at 46 years, 177 days. Teddy Roosevelt (1901–09) is the youngest president at 42 years, 322 days. He had the career good fortune, like millions of workers around the world, of his boss leaving the office earlier than expected.[7]

The oldest president to take office for the first time is Trump at 70 years, 220 days. Reagan is second at 69 years, 349 days. Reagan remains for now the oldest president after reaching one month short of 78 at the end of his second term.

Based on national actuarial tables for similar ages, a paper from the American Federation for Aging Research gave Biden at least a 79.2 per cent four-year survival probability from the 2021 inauguration and Donald Trump 84.8 per cent. That changes to 70 per cent for a second-term Biden. No figures were given for a third-term Trump, which would, of course, be unconstitutional. The federation stressed these figures were not based on the health conditions of the individuals themselves and rightly said that 'chronological age should not be a relevant criterion used to judge presidential candidates' – and I apologise for endless age-related references in this book.[8]

Rush for Power
Most presidents have been in their 50s on winning power, with 25 of them so far. Only one, Trump, has been in his 70s, with 10 in their 60s and nine in their 40s. The figures for presidential age include Cleveland winning at ages 47 and 55, officially making him the No. 22 (1885–89) and the No. 24 president (1893–97) because he held two non-consecutive terms. Any constitutional amendment to remove all mention of the G-man would be most welcome.

Nobody has ever won in their 30s, meaning age 35 or more under the constitutional requirement, and it's one of the last remaining challenges in American politics, along with winning – or losing – every state. William Jennings Bryan lost 271-176 to McKinley as the Democratic presidential candidate in 1896 at age 36, and lost 292-155 in a rematch with McKinley in 1900. A legend in his own Electoral College, Bryan was 48 when he ran for a third time and lost 321-162 against Taft in 1908. That left him with 493 electoral votes from three attempts.

Vice presidents reached the 30s landmark as far back as 1857. Buchanan's running mate, John C. Breckinridge, was only 36 years old when the 12-letter Kentuckian became the 14th vice president. Nixon had just turned 40 on becoming vice president in January 1953. A key difference to presidential candidates is that Veeps have regularly been selected by the candidate and sometimes comparative youth is a specific attraction. The 41-year-old Dan Quayle ran with 64-year-old George H. W. Bush on the winning 1988 Republican ticket, though being seen as a reliable conservative from Indiana, like current Vice President Mike Pence, was probably more important. Pence was born in 1959.

The first president to be born in the 19th century was Franklin Pierce, born in 1804, though a later president, Millard Fillmore (1850–53), was born in 1800. JFK, born in 1917, was the first president in office to be born in the 20th century. LBJ was born in 1908 but followed Kennedy in the White House.

October Surprise

The biggest age transition from one president to another is around 27 years when the 43-year-old Kennedy took over from the 70-year-old Eisenhower in 1961. Ike had thought

JFK too inexperienced; Kennedy had seen Eisenhower as too stuffy.

The biggest age difference between two major Democratic and Republican candidates is when Barack Obama (b. 1961) took on John McCain (b. 1936). Obama was 25 days short of being exactly 25 years younger than McCain. As often happens, the older candidate was the genuine maverick.

A record six presidents have been born in October – John Adams, Hayes, Chester A. Arthur, Teddy Roosevelt, Eisenhower and Carter – followed by August and November. Only one president, Taft, was born in September, but he was likely a big baby. No president has been born on Christmas Day or the Fourth of July, though Founding Fathers John Adams, Jefferson and Monroe all died on Independence Day, the first two in 1826 on the 50th anniversary of the Declaration of Independence.

The most common day of the month for a president to be born on is the 29th, with four presidents (Tyler, Andrew Johnson, McKinley and JFK), followed by three each on the 4th, 14th and 27th. William Henry Harrison, the ninth president, was born on 9 February, likewise Wilson entered this world on the 28th (December) and is the 28th president. Harrison wins on a toss-up, with Wilson's number divisible by 2, 4, 7 and 14.

Get ready for the wacky world of presidential trivia.

Presidential Trivia

Prime Time
Even Amazon's state-of-the-art algorithms would express wonder at the fact that every prime-number president

since the 1868 election has been Republican, including William Henry Harrison's grandson.

The long list started with No. 19, Hayes, and No. 23, Benjamin Harrison, who cleverly won the Electoral College vote in 1888 with the prime number of 233 despite losing the popular vote to Cleveland. After him, No. 29, Harding, No. 31, Hoover, No. 37, Nixon, No. 41, George H. W. Bush, and No. 43, George W. Bush, with another prime number of 271 electoral votes, kept the show on the road. The next prime number is 47 – the president after Biden or two after Trump.

Electrical engineering professor Aziz Inan took advantage of Kennedy's centennial in 2017 to note: 'JFK's 100th birthday, May 29, was the 149th day of 2017, where 149 is the 35th prime number. Coincidentally, JFK served as the 35th U.S. President.'[9]

High Hopes
It's clear that voters focus on far more important matters than a candidate's eligibility to be a prime-number president.

Like their height, weight, hair and star sign.

Biden is 6 feet tall, and three or perhaps two inches smaller than Trump. The average height of U.S. presidents is around 5'11".[10] Lincoln, said to take three steps at a time, is the tallest president so far at 6'4". One magazine calculated that 'in the 28 elections between 1900 and 2011, the taller candidate has won 18 times, while the shorter has won just eight', with two draws.[11] That calculation appears to award Eisenhower the height advantage over Stevenson in the Battle of the Baldies (see below) in 1952 and 1956, but both elections may have squeaked in as draws depending on your tape measure. The Eisenhower

Library puts Ike at 5'10" – others add a half-inch, as you do. Stevenson is also believed to have been 5'10", so we have a dilemma and coronavirus makes any requests for exhumation extremely insensitive. If we do call those two elections a draw, that makes it 10 times the tallest candidate has won, and only five to the shortest, for the 18 elections post-Second World War. The three draws include the 1992 race between George H. W. Bush and Bill Clinton.

Some wins have been clear judged by height. The 6'3" LBJ beat 5'11" Goldwater, and George H. W. Bush beat Michael Dukakis 6'2" to 5'8". John Kerry, George W. Bush's Democratic opponent in 2004, would have risen to the heights of Lincoln at 6'4" if he had won. He did not.

Trump Towers

That brings us to the 6'3" Trump's win over Hillary Clinton and a potentially new low in presidential politics, with both candidates taking cover from incoming fire over their height.

Hillary Clinton's height has reportedly varied between 5'5" and 5'7", perhaps by standing on a stack of printed emails. One presidential height chronicler said the 2008 Hillary campaign, which fell short of clinching the nomination, put their candidate at 5'5", and the same writer also noted that Trump could be exaggerating his height.[12]

Many have doubts over Trump. Ian Crouch wondered in *The New Yorker* if 'perhaps his height had been boosted an inch or two by his antigravity coiffure, or his weight shaved off by a pound or twenty', possibly to avoid an obesity label.[13] The same article discussed 'the rise of the anti-Trump "Girthers"', noting that MSNBC host Chris Hayes had come up with the term. It's a witty reference to the Trump-encouraged 'Birther' movement which (wrongly) claimed Barack Obama had not been born in the U.S. but in Kenya, making him ineligible for the presidency.

Trump didn't come down to earth on the Birther conspiracy theory for years, and former First Lady Michelle Obama will reportedly 'never forgive' him for it. Barack Obama, blessed with Reagan's self-deprecatory humour, said in 2012 on *The Tonight Show with Jay Leno* that 'this all dates back to when we were growing up together in Kenya'. To wild applause, Obama added that he and Trump 'had constant run-ins on the soccer field [and] he wasn't very good'. That's how to run against Trump.

Bald and Beautiful
Trump fascinates on many levels, including the top floor.

Trump's troubled thatch continues to amuse many observers, with *Vanity Fair* comparing it to 'a dead, furry lobster', although Biden, to use brutal Bentsen debate lingo, 'is no Jack Kennedy'.[14] Baldness doesn't help win elections, but it's not very useful for comparison anyway. It depends where you draw the line. Two-time winner Eisenhower in the 1950s is generally considered to be the last bald president. Eisenhower's two-time opponent Adlai Stevenson was also almost completely gone (hair-wise). JFK restored the natural order with his bountiful locks, but hair-challenged Ford struggled with more than an economic recession and lost to Carter in 1976. In the modern age of TV and social media, a good mop on top is a big plus for candidates.

How about beards and moustaches?

Lincoln grew a beard without the moustache after receiving a letter from 11-year-old Grace Bedell recommending some whiskers, but beards and moustaches have long been a total no-no for modern presidents. The last President Hairy Face was Taft (1909–13), who attracted praise from GQ in 2016 for his moustache's 'hell of a curlicue'.[15] Tom Dewey, damagingly called 'the little man on the wedding cake' by Alice Roosevelt Longworth, had a moustache for his 1944 defeat to FDR and bravely kept it for his loss to Truman in 1948.

2020 Vision

Truman (1945–53) is the last president to regularly wear spectacles in public, not counting reading glasses.[16]

The 1964 Republican candidate Goldwater wore black horn-rim glasses. He was always considered ahead of his time by fellow conservatives, finally having his revenge with Reagan's election 16 years later, and Specsavers says 'these vintage-style glasses are swinging right back into fashion'.

Goldwater was thrashed by LBJ, who also wore glasses in public on occasion. He did not do so when sworn in on Air Force One shortly after Kennedy's assassination, but the glasses were on show in his first address to the Joint Session of Congress on 27 November 1963 when he told the world: 'All I have I would have given gladly not to be standing here today.'

The specs stayed on for the momentous 1964 State of the Union address in which Johnson asked for massive advances in civil rights and called for 'all-out war on human poverty and unemployment in these United States'. LBJ wore no glasses in the 1965 State of the Union but they looked on during his shock TV announcement in

March 1968 that he would not stand for president again and instead focus on the Vietnam War.

Third-party irritant Ross Perot wore glasses in his 1992 and 1996 campaigns.

In the Stars

Presidents' Day in America is the third Monday in February. It especially honours Washington, who was born 22 February, or 11 February under the old Julian calendar, and Lincoln, born 12 February.

Biden is a Scorpio, born on 20 November, while 14 June baby Trump is a Gemini like JFK and George H. W. Bush, neither of whom served a second term.

Scorpio and Aquarius, which includes Lincoln, have provided the most presidents so far at five each. But Aquarius has won more than twice the number of elections as Scorpio – 11 to a miserable 5.[17] Aquarius presidents are McKinley, born 29 January, who won twice; FDR, 30 January, an eternal four wins; Reagan, 6 February, two wins; William Henry Harrison, 9 February, only one; and double-winner Lincoln. Scorpio presidents are Teddy Roosevelt (27 October), John Adams (30 October), Polk (2 November), Harding (2 November) and Garfield (19 November). All won one election with plenty of caveats. Polk had committed himself to one term only, Harding and Garfield died in office, and Roosevelt could have been re-elected in 1908 if he had chosen to run. If he wins, Biden will be the first Scorpio to win an election since Harding (1921–23), who was born in 1865.

Aries (Jefferson and Tyler) and Virgo (Taft and LBJ) have the fewest presidents. Shockingly, no Piscean has won a presidential election since Grover Cleveland in 1893.[18]

Going for Gold

Three of the top four U.S. Olympic gold medal hauls have come in years which saw Republicans win the presidential election: 83 golds in Los Angeles in 1984 when Reagan was re-elected; 79 golds in St Louis in 1904, an easy win for Teddy Roosevelt; and 46 in Rio de Janeiro in 2016 ahead of Trump's triumph. The U.S. also got 46 golds in London in 2012 when Obama won a second term.

LBJ is the only president whose number exactly matches as the 36th president with 36 U.S. golds in 1964. Both Trump, No. 45 and 46 golds in 2016, and Kennedy, No. 35 and 34 golds in 1960, were one medal out. That could be Trump's last chance, with the 2020 Tokyo Games postponed by a year due to coronavirus. Statistically speaking, it's possible for the future 48th American president to see the U.S. win 48 golds in '48. No. 45 Trump would have to win a second term, followed by two-term presidents in 2025–33 (No. 46), 2033–41 (No. 47) and 2041–49 (No. 48).

Ahead of Los Angeles 2028, America has hosted four Summer Olympics with the incumbent president winning three of those years: Teddy Roosevelt in 1904, Reagan in 1984, and Clinton in 1996 (Atlanta). FDR ousted Herbert Hoover after the 1932 LA Games.

The men's 100-metre world record is also one to keep an eye on, wherever it happens. A record time has been set at least once in 12 presidential election years, including Usain Bolt's 9.72 and 9.69 in 2008 before his 9.58 mark the following year. The Democratic candidate has gone on to win eight of those 12 years, in 2008, 1996, 1964, 1960, 1948, 1936, 1932 and 1912, and the Republicans four, in 1988, 1968, 1956 and 1920.[19]

Ding-dongs

The European Football Championship usually takes place in the same year as presidential elections. That's very helpful. The footballing feast has been postponed in 2020 due to coronavirus. That's not very helpful.

Spain is very much the team to watch for the Democrats, and Germany for the Republicans. Spain's three Euro trophies all came in years which later saw Democratic candidates win: 1964 (LBJ), 2008 and 2012 (both Obama). Spain lost the final in 1984 and so did the Democratic candidate Mondale. It's arguable that Mondale would have been annihilated by Reagan even if Spain had won 10-0 but we shall never know.

It's a perfect 4/4 record – Spain wins the final, Democrats win the presidency. Spain loses, Democrats lose. Unfortunately for Biden, we won't know what any of this retrospectively means until 2021 when the postponed 2020 Euros finally take place, though it may help the Spanish football team in advance.

West Germany and Nixon thumped the Soviet Union and left-leaning George McGovern 3-0 and 520-17 respectively in 1972. The West Germans and Ford lost in 1976 to Panenka's penalty and Nixon's presidential pardon, before the 1980 victory saw Reagan replace Ford up front. A now unified Germany lost the final in 1992 (Clinton) and 2008 (Obama), two years where Republicans also lost. The perfect record is only ruined by Germany and Clinton winning in 1996 for an overall 5/6 score.

The Republic of France is also good for the Republicans, with wins in 1984 and 2000 (George W. Bush), but it let Trump down with a 1-0 loss to Portugal in 2016 after extra time.

In another competition also not taking place in 2020, no Democratic candidate has ever lost a presidential election the year after the Netherlands won the Eurovision Song Contest. Teddy Scholten's 1959 winning entry led to Kennedy taking the White House by *Een beetje* (a little bit) against Nixon. Carter came out on top in his *Ding-a-dong* with Ford after Teach-In won in 1975.

Switzerland has twice come first in Republican-winning years, 1956 and 1988. Celine Dion was the winner in the latter year – of the song contest, that is.

Having a Laugh

Finally, does the animal world tell us anything?

Not really.

Carter is the only president to have the letters for 'cat' in his name, which is hard to believe but true, and Coolidge the sole 'dog'. Carter has also been a 'rat' alongside Truman, Arthur, Grant, Taylor and Nixon (honorary membership).

Lincoln and Clinton belong to the exclusive 'lion' club but Jackson deserves special mention after refusing the gift of an actual lion from the Emperor of Morocco and telling Congress to handle the matter.[20]

Eisenhower remains the only 'horse' to ride to the White House.

Out of the 44 different American presidents so far, it's the 6-footer President Garfield who comes closest to having a 'giraffe'. Garfield's last name is forever lacking the extra 'f' in one of presidential animal wordplay's greatest tragedies.

Triple Whammy

So what have we learnt?

Trump has the chance for a White House Triple Whammy as the first five-letter Republican president to serve a full two terms since Grant in the 1870s, the first-ever Gemini to be re-elected and, if he survives any second-term impeachment over mass Dettol poisonings, the oldest-ever president.

Only Biden can stop him unless, as we see in the next chapter, the Electoral College behaves exceptionally badly.

4

O Ye of Little Fish: Problems with the Electoral College

Jimmy Carter was curious. In the early days of a longshot bid for the White House, the future 39th president (1977–81) was keen for any chance to spread his message as he chased the Democratic nomination.

So why was his own press secretary, Jody Powell, being infuriatingly secretive as the two men headed for a TV studio early one morning? Showing the attention to detail which would later earn him unkind mockery as president, including the claim that he read and vetted the White House tennis court schedule, Carter wouldn't be silenced.[1]

'(Carter) asked "What kind of programme is it?" and Powell would not answer him. Then Carter asked him again more sternly, "What kind of programme is it?" and Powell answered him with a question, "Do you have any favourite recipes?"' At this point Powell confessed to his boss that the former governor of Georgia and would-be president of the United States was about to appear on a cooking show where Carter 'had to share his favourite rough fish cooking recipe'.[2]

Politicians do things they wouldn't always be comfortable doing in the race for the party nomination, and the intense concentration on key states sets a bad precedent. As candidates dream of becoming leader of all Americans, they absorb the notion that the way to achieve this is to ignore a huge chunk of them. And that's a problem with the Electoral College.[3]

Look Up

Even a conscientious and hard-working campaigner like Carter wasn't above the selective approach: 'According to figures compiled by Jimmy Carter's campaign in 1976, 11 states did not receive a single visit during the general election campaign from either Carter or his vice-presidential running mate, while 12 other states received just one visit.'[4]

Ignored states can be very small and not worth the effort, or large and too safe, with insufficient incentive for candidates to pay a visit given the limited time and resources available. But there is the traditional belief that the Electoral College protects smaller states. Professor Robert M. Alexander, a leading contemporary scholar of the Electoral College, notes that defenders of the current system 'argue that without the Electoral College, campaigns would only take place in urban areas, with great attention devoted to states such as New York and California'. Alexander adds that in an interview with a presidential elector 'one told me that "without the Electoral College, all we'd see is the underside of his (the candidate's) plane on his way to New York or California – if you have a set of binoculars"'.[5]

That's one danger to keep in mind as we look at the biggest criticism of the Electoral College: Winners sometimes lose.

And the Winner Isn't...

An increasing problem with the Electoral College is that the problem is increasing. Up until the 21st century, professors, politicians and pundits could point out dozens of theoretical pitfalls and constitutional dead-ends that the Electoral College threatened to take America down. However, they knew – and, much more importantly, so did the voters – that there would nearly always be a clear winner coming out of Election Day.

What's changed is that an unusual 'undemocratic' result threatens to become a regular outcome, and, in the Land of the Free, that's a problem. In wider American society there's understandable unrest in the air. Faithless electors could become a powerful conduit for change by refusing to play the game in a close presidential election should the winner again get fewer popular votes than the loser. If faithless electors dared to go as far as ignoring the same winner for both the popular and electoral vote because enough of them just didn't like that winner, this would almost certainly kill the Electoral College. Its biggest strength – the rules are known and applied – props up its biggest weakness – it can be an unfair game to start with.

Shout-out for Shootout

America has been led down the standard 'Winner loses-Loser wins' path at least five times – 1824, 1876, 1888, 2000 and 2016 – where the candidate with the most popular votes does not have enough electoral votes to become president when all the electors meet in their individual states. That's possibly six times if popular votes extrapolated from unpledged Alabama voters in the

1960 election are removed from Kennedy's total, making Richard Nixon the popular vote winner but JFK still president.

The first time, 1824, demands a special shout-out for Andrew Jackson, a tough duelling military man not to be rifled or trifled with. Trump is a fan, and hung his portrait in the Oval Office. Jackson, who treated Native Americans abysmally, is the only candidate to have lost despite winning both the popular vote and Electoral College vote (without getting a majority), which he did in the 1824 election.

Informing him of that defeat would get into history's top five most difficult jobs. Jackson took things personally: 'In 1806, an argument over a horse race – the dispute also apparently included a slur against (his wife) Rachel – degenerated into a duel between Jackson and a man in Nashville named Charles Dickinson.' Jackson was shot in the chest before killing his enemy, and 'carried Dickinson's bullet in his body until he died'.[6] The bullet wouldn't be alone for too long.[7]

Jackson, a key figure in the history of the Democratic Party, made up for the 1824 loss with victories in 1828 and 1832.

Ways to Lose

Candidate A wins the popular vote in November. Candidate B wins the presidency when all the electoral votes are cast in December and counted in January by Congress.

As we've seen, this hasn't happened too often over the 58 elections so far but it has occurred enough to cause concern. It threatens to become a regular occurrence in the 21st century, having happened in 2000 and 2016 and looming as a possibility in 2020, so it could become a crisis.

An even greater sense of outrage would be caused by Candidate A winning the popular vote in November, securing a majority at the Electoral College in December but losing the official count in January if some state votes were challenged and not accepted. It's complicated, it's unlikely, but the many possible endings show weaknesses in the process. It all perhaps helps to explain why 'no aspect of the American system is less understood and more bewildering than the Electoral College'.[8]

Don't get the wrong idea. Nowadays the next president is usually known on Election Night itself, though 20 years back Florida dragged on to 13 December when Al Gore conceded for the second time (see 2000 election in Chapter 7) and said of Bush: 'I promised that I wouldn't call him back this time.' Gore, not typically given to wit, had conceded on Election Night itself before changing his mind as his position improved in Florida.[9]

There is one dramatic but far-from-far-fetched example which could keep the whole world awake except for the individual concerned: Candidate A wins the popular vote in November, Candidate A secures a majority of the electoral votes in December, Candidate A sends Candidate B season's greetings, Candidate A wins the official count in January, Candidate A drops dead before Inauguration Day.

In the music industry, this would be titled *Now that's what I call a problem*.

Late Riser

Death is the big glaring hole in the ground for the Electoral College. If there's any golden rule to campaigning, it's this: Don't die (or resign). It gets really complicated. So much so that a great guide to the Electoral College, *After the People Vote*, devotes a whole chapter to the question, 'What If a Major Party Candidate Dies or Resigns?'[10] This is a genuinely admirable book and a must-read for all morticians who pride themselves on following current affairs.

Apart from the four assassinations (Lincoln 1865, Garfield 1881, McKinley 1901, JFK 1963), four presidents have fallen ill in office and died. They were William Henry Harrison in 1841, cherry-guzzling Zachary Taylor in 1850 and Warren 'matchless breasts' Harding in 1923, and polio-stricken presidential great Franklin Delano Roosevelt in 1945.[11] In a final service to their country, all eight have died outside of electorally sensitive timeframes.

That may not always be the case.

What Would Happen?

There are four distinct phases to the 2020 presidential election: 1) before ordinary Americans vote on Election Day on 3 November; 2) between Election Day and the presidential electors meeting to vote on 14 December; 3) between the electors meeting and Congress officially counting their votes on 6 January; and 4) between Congress counting and Inauguration Day on 20 January.[12]

It's not a simple process to start with, so consider all this going on amidst a shock death and a bad-tempered campaign which had produced a controversial result and huge unrest in the country. Florida 2000 gave us an appalling glimpse of what to expect.

The No. 1 stage is the clearest. Where a candidate calls it earthly quits before Election Day they'll be replaced on the ticket by a name put forward by the Democratic

National Committee (DNC) or Republican National Committee (RNC) after consultations within the party. If only the rest were so simple. Read on if you've got a quiet week ahead.

Dearly Departed

What about problems at the second stage, if a candidate contests the November election but dies before the electors meet in December? 'This is the messiest situation and could unleash a lot of different manoeuvres and disputes,' election expert Richard Pildes told *The Washington Post*.[13]

A new candidate, probably the vice presidential nominee, would be chosen by the party hierarchy and thrown into the mix for the presidential electors to decide. That won't matter if the party has lost the November election, as was the case for the Democrats in 1872. However, if it knows it has won the election, the party is effectively naming the next president with the dead candidate's electors constitutionally free to vote for the new presidential candidate. The author apologises in advance if he's completely misunderstood – let's be frank, it wouldn't be the first time.

What happens if a death occurs at phase three, after the electors have met but before their votes have been officially opened and counted in Washington? In one scenario, 'Congress could choose to count the votes for the deceased or resigned presidential candidate, thereby making him or her the president-elect (even if deceased)' with the vice president-elect then being sworn in as president on Inauguration Day under Section 3 of the Twentieth Amendment.[14]

After the People Vote adds that if Congress didn't accept the votes, and there is therefore no official president-elect, and nobody with a majority, the winner could end up being decided by the House of Representatives in what's known as a contingent election. This involves the top three from the November election, one of whom at the very, very least is pretending to be dead by my reckoning.

In the last and comparatively much clearer stage: win the official count in January and become president-elect but die before Inauguration Day in January, and the vice president-elect will be inaugurated as president under the Twentieth Amendment.

That's enough.

When in Missouri

While you can't posthumously wing it into presidential power, rather unfairly you can go down in a plane crash and still get chosen for the United States Senate by the kind folks of the state of Missouri three weeks later. Democratic candidate Mel C – not the Spice Girl but Mel Carnahan – did just this in the 2000 Senate elections.

Exasperated Republicans saw Carnahan's approval ratings rise after his plane crashed in Missouri forest with his pilot son Randy at the controls. Some hid their grief well to argue that Carnahan was no longer an inhabitant of the state and so not eligible to hold office.[15] Republican candidate John Ashcroft, later a controversial U.S. Attorney General, lost to the late Carnahan, whose wife, Jean Carnahan, was appointed by the (living) governor to serve for two years.

No dead person has ever ended up president, though Thomas Jefferson successfully pleaded from the grave for his White House years to be kept off his headstone. America's third Chief Magistrate, as presidents used to be called, left instructions for the listing of three achievements and 'not a word more'. 'Author of the Declaration of American Independence' made the cut, but Jefferson's successful 1801–09 presidency failed to get a look in. Jefferson's other two inscribed achievements are his authorship of the 'Statute of Virginia for religious freedom' and 'Father of the University of Virginia'.

Faithless Electors

Faithless electors are potentially the sleeping assassins within the system, able to bring the Electoral College to its knees at any time. They're the ones who can decide not to back the candidate the voters have supported.

More than 30 states have procedures for spanking faithless electors in various ways and places but the issue was seemingly decided by a U.S. Supreme Court unanimous ruling in July 2020 which eased mostly Republican fears over any 2020 naughtiness. The very fact the Supremes discussed the issue was a sure sign of its growing importance.

Can the states punish electors who don't do as they're told? Yes. Justice Clarence Thomas appeared sympathetic, like others on the (virtual) bench. He observed that 'electors would be free to vote for anyone they wanted without recourse including Frodo Baggins', Tolkien's famous hobbit in *The Lord of the Rings*.[16]

The Supreme Court ruling could finally put the constitutional lid on the centuries-old issue of faithless electors by allowing, even forcing, states to intervene where necessary. That said, the proof will be in the pudding. Americans aren't too keen on being told what to do so don't be too surprised if Thomas' throwaway but serious remark ends up with a faithless elector voting for Frodo.

Congress would intervene if Frodo ended up president, if only on the grounds that it wouldn't be easy finding a vice president, but there's a serious principle at stake here. The electors – faithful or not – were formally hired by the Constitution in the first place. They were placed at the heart of the process of choosing the president in order to keep things in order. That they haven't done so is not the point – it's what potential future consequence there might be by taking away this constitutional deterrent.

For some observers, faithless electors are doing what the Founding Fathers wanted them to do. Robert Bennett sees the irony in the situation: 'What are today called "faithless electors" are those who abstain or vote for a candidate other than the one to whom they were pledged. The "faithlessness" is to their pledges. The irony is that it is only they who are faithful to at least a part of the original conception of how the electors were to decide on the presidency of the United States.'[17]

Wicked parties quickly perverted the voting system into making sure their candidate won, including the system of 'winner takes all' for electoral votes in a state, instead of splitting them according to the share of the vote. The original intention was to have electors meet in their own states to discuss and choose the best candidate. There was the double safety net that, if all the individual states couldn't come up collectively with a winner, the House of Representatives would make the final call on a best for America basis (or best for white male Americans) with each state delegation having one vote.

Mountains, Molehills

Even if you don't like faithless electors, the problem shouldn't be over-exaggerated: 'Over the course of American history, less than 1 per cent of all electors have voted contrary to expectations. And while faithless electors did force the Senate to choose the vice president in 1836, they have never changed the outcome of a presidential race.'[18]

Fairvote.org, which is a 'non-partisan champion of electoral reforms', gives a list of the faithless presidential electors through time, with a significant occasion being 1872 when Horace Greeley died after losing the election to Ulysses S. Grant but before the electors had met. Altogether 63 votes were distributed among others in what for some is technically not a display of faithlessness since death is involved.

Significantly, the only other double-digit show of faithless voters was, wait for it, at the last election in 2016. Hence nerves before the court ruling if a similar result occurs in 2020 where the popular vote winner loses the electoral vote. The smaller the electoral margin of victory, the bigger the temptation for an outbreak of faithlessness. 'Following the 2016 presidential election, 10 electors attempted to cast ballots for candidates other than those to whom they were pledged; seven succeeded. Three Clinton-Kaine electors – from Colorado, Maine, and Minnesota – attempted to vote for other candidates, but they were replaced by alternates who cast their ballots as electors according to the voters' preference.'[19]

Clinton lost four votes in the state of Washington and one in Hawaii, and Trump lost two in Texas. None of it mattered then, but all of it could. Picture electors meeting in December 2020 with one candidate leading the other by a handful of votes. Faithless electors could suddenly get itchy fingers. The Supreme Court ruling, which involved laws in Colorado and Washington, likely put a stop to all that with a lockdown on misbehaviour.

National Popular Vote

Some modern issues would flummox the Founding Fathers, such as self-driving cars and Elvis Week in August. Other issues are essentially the same today as they were in the 1780s, just slightly shook up, including the idea of a straight national vote for president.

The National Popular Vote Interstate Compact is smart, radical and poses a growing threat to voting traditionalists. It keeps the Electoral College but ensures the elected president can never again get into office without winning the most votes on Election Day.

How would it work? A number of states with combined control of 270-plus electoral votes agree in advance to give all these votes to the candidate who wins the popular vote nationally, regardless of the actual individual state result. The NPV would see a compact member state like California giving its 55 electoral votes to a Republican with the most popular votes overall in the country, even if a Democrat had got every single vote from every living Californian. This way every vote in the country counts and candidates would know they had to win the popular vote as well, with all the consequences that has for campaign strategy.

Depending on the rules agreed, the first election with the Interstate Compact in operation could be tense, for example if a member state also had a vote on the same Election Day to repeal the compact applying to that state.

Overall, it's a politically savvy way of keeping state voting identities while ensuring a genuine popular winner, and safeguards will be built into the system. If it worked just once, the switch to a straightforward direct vote abolishing the Electoral College might be the result.

More Mo

What did LBJ say? Learn to count. Mid-2020, the non-partisan National Popular Vote Inc. behind the campaign says 15 states and Washington, D.C., with a total of 196 electoral votes, have signed up. Crucially, the campaign has politics' vital ingredient for success: momentum, or 'The Big Mo', with Connecticut, Colorado, Delaware, New Mexico and Oregon recent additions. They're not an awful long way off the magic number of 270 needed to win an election, though three big states – California, New York (29) and Illinois (20) – are already part of the compact.

Having a president with a direct democratic mandate has cropped up as a frequent suggestion through the centuries, usually without the Electoral College. This came from a progress report in 1964: 'The plan for direct election of the President was given serious consideration at the Constitutional Convention. Defeated, it was nonetheless revised in 1826 in the form of a constitutional amendment and has since been proposed in over 90 legislative bills.'[20]

Lots of Horses

A genuine national race would make it easier for good and bad candidates alike to take part. That has problems of its own. Adding lots more horses to the traditional two-horse race makes it far harder for anyone to get a majority, calling into question the legitimacy of the winner's mandate. The super-rich could (almost) run for fun.

One serious candidate, former New York Mayor Michael Bloomberg, could well have gone the distance in the 2020 race if the option of bypassing the Democratic nomination had been available to him. He was possibly the opponent Trump feared most, judging by the torrent of derogatory tweets about 'Mini-Mike'. One reason Bloomberg worried Trump so much was his financial status, shown by Bloomberg's withering answer to concerns that the election could be a battle of billionaires: 'Who's the other billionaire?' he asked CNN's Christiane Amanpour.

Donald Trump considered bids in 1988 and 2000. He might have gone the whole way and run for president in these years under a National Popular Vote arrangement, but that's unsupported conjecture by the author (see rest of book).

Your Choice

Just as faithless electors are allowed to be, well, faithless, states are constitutionally allowed to decide how electors are chosen, and originally some state legislatures opted to choose electors themselves rather than let the people do it. Article II, Section 1 of the U.S. Constitution partly reads, 'Each State shall appoint, in such Manner as the Legislature thereof may direct, A Number of Electors.'

But critics say NPV is cleverly using the Constitution to bypass the Constitution and any need for a time-consuming constitutional amendment, which needs the backing of two-thirds of the House of Representatives and the Senate, as well as the approval of 38 states. It would be a massive change to how America votes and, if the movement continues to make waves and attract more states, the issue will surely end up with the Supreme Court, where all bets are off.

There have also been suggestions to have priority voting with candidates rated in preference (this is criticised as being complicated, as if the Electoral College isn't) or to share electoral votes within a state, which would be easy to do and also have a major effect on campaigns and results. Electoral votes awarded by a state could reflect final percentages across the state, or split the state into a series of separate races and electoral prizes. Maine and Nebraska, the only two states with electoral votes linked to districts within the states, have shown that tweaks aren't so terrible. It can be done.

Reasons for Believing

Apart from book sales, why keep the Electoral College? Well, Americans are used to it, it generally produces clear choices for president, all sides know the rules and, just to be clear, book sales are very important.

If you switch to NPV, why wait until January for the president to take office? Overnight inaugurations would have a knock-on effect on other elections in November, or you risk ending up with a new president with an old congress, and not for the first time.

A big objection to NPV is what to do if you have a big objection. In the Electoral College, election disputes and dissent have been localised, albeit with a huge significance for the final national result. Under NPV, the ultimate nightmare scenario would be a close race and a national recount. They're exaggerated fears, but it's best to be prepared.

The Electoral College has been a major weapon in America's political tradition of parties peacefully exchanging control of the presidency, but it will face a fight for survival if it misfires yet again in 2020. If more states start to believe the Electoral College has stopped working, it risks being sent to the repair shop or thrown away for good.

5

Father of the Nation to Uncle Abe
1789–1864

This chapter is bookmarked by America's two greatest presidents – Washington and Abraham Lincoln. 'Father of His Country' Washington almost certainly did not chop down that fabled cherry tree as a child but did lead the emerging United States to independence as an adult. Uncle Abe, who chopped wood when young, saved the Union and axed slavery in his 50s. The 16th president would never see his 60s.

Out of the 44 presidents (Grover Cleveland annoyingly counts twice with non-consecutive terms), Washington is the only one not to have lived in the actual White House. Why? They hadn't finished building it. While he 'had selected the site for the White House and approved its design, he never lived' in the president's Executive Mansion in the capital named in his honour.[1]

The population in 1790 was just under four million, which included 697,681 slaves who obviously couldn't vote. Reynolds points out that even the largest 'city', Philadelphia, was home to no more than 50,000 people.[2]

The first presidential election was in 1789 when up to 13 states had their first shot at the Electoral College experiment. In order of admission to the Union, along with their nicknames, they were: 'First State' Delaware (1st, 1787), 'Keystone State' Pennsylvania (2nd, 1787), 'Garden State' New Jersey (3rd, 1787), 'Peach State' Georgia (4th, 1788), 'Constitution State' Connecticut (5th, 1788), 'Bay State' Massachusetts (6th, 1788), 'Old Line State' Maryland (7th, 1788), 'Always Causing Trouble State' South Carolina (8th, 1788), 'Granite State' New Hampshire (9th, 1788), 'Old Dominion' Virginia (10th, 1788), 'Empire State' New York (11th, 1788), 'Tarheel State' North Carolina (12th, 1789) and 'Ocean State' Rhode Island (13th, 1790).[3]

This chapter includes four hugely significant elections in American history with major consequences for the country: 1800, when power passed peacefully between rival parties for the first time; 1824, when Andrew Jackson was the only candidate to be denied victory despite getting the most popular and electoral votes; 1860, which put Lincoln in charge of America's fate in the Civil War; and 1864, which kept Lincoln in power.

It's arguable that only 1876, a heavily disputed election not long after the Civil War, and 1932, bringing Franklin Delano Roosevelt to power to tackle the Great Depression, rival these four elections. Because of that, this will be more of a slog than the following two election chapters. The author would like to wish readers all the best.

1789 Election

Washington is the only president to have been chosen unanimously by presidential electors. Twice. In the very first election in 1789, Washington received the support of all 69 electors who voted and John Adams was selected as his vice president on 34 votes.[4] Only 10 states ended up taking part; internal squabbles in New York prevented any vote, and North Carolina and Rhode Island were yet to ratify the Constitution.

Washington was inaugurated on 30 April 1789 on the balcony of New York's original Federal Hall (demolished in 1812). He set the tradition of taking the oath on a Bible, in his case 'opened at random due to haste to Genesis 49:13'.[5]

Under the Constitution, each elector originally had two votes for president, rather than one for president and one for vice president when the 12th Amendment was later added. In the Electoral College's first outing, presidential votes were spread among a dozen names, such as one for the unrelated Benjamin Lincoln (no relation to Abe – or the author). This wasn't against the spirit of the Constitution – quite the contrary – but gave a strong hint that the Electoral College would turn out to be unpredictable.

1792 Election

Washington again won unanimously in 1792, with 132 votes, but there would never be a non-partisan presidential election ever again.

Federalist Adams got 77 votes and remained vice president, ahead of George Clinton on 50 for a disgruntled group of Democratic-Republicans. The Federalist faction/party, whose most enthusiastic proponent was Treasury Secretary Alexander Hamilton, favoured a strong central government, a national bank and stable relations with former owner Britain. In contrast, France-loving Jefferson had a thing for farmers and led the

Democratic-Republicans – everyone was a republican, the stress was on the democratic side – who believed states knew best.

'Hamilton, of New York, had no love for popular democracy: he wanted a society in which property (above all moneyed paper-property) was secure and propertied men had the greatest weight,' Lionel Elvin wrote in England during the Second World War in a book dedicated 'To my wife and son in America'. The contrast was clear for Elvin: 'Jefferson, coming from rural Virginia, wanted to fuse existing frontier democracy with abstract egalitarian ideas'.[6] The nub of these early arguments has never truly gone away.

Fifteen states voted in total, including 'Green Mountain State' Vermont (the 14th state to join the Union, in 1791) and 'Bluegrass State' Kentucky (15th, 1792).

Washington had not been keen on a second term after an exhausting life in service of his country. He delivered the shortest inaugural address at 135 words, a record which still holds, this time in the Senate Chamber of Philadelphia's Congress Hall. Washington had gotten used to traveling and America was used to swapping capitals.[7]

1796 Election

It was not yet used to swapping presidents. Washington wouldn't stand for a third time, thereby setting a powerful two-term tradition which was ended as late as 1940 by Franklin Delano Roosevelt – the only president to challenge Washington and Lincoln at the top of the presidential charts – with much of the world at war.

Vice President Adams came first in 1796 with 71 electoral votes and his opponent Jefferson second with 68, including the support of 'Volunteer State' Tennessee

(16th, 1796). The next administration would have a president and vice president from different parties.

It was a curious situation. 'Not only was it the first transition to a new president, it was also the only case where the two main rivals had essentially *both* won and now had to move in to office together.'[8]

Samuel Miles of Pennsylvania became America's first 'faithless elector' after backing Jefferson over Adams, sparking protests and 'prompting the much-quoted voter's remark that Miles had been chosen "to act, not to think"'.[9]

1800 Election

The 1800 election crashed the Electoral College party, triggering an urgent reboot, after Jefferson and his intended vice president Aaron Burr both finished top on 73 votes, which gave Burr an idea above his station.

The often brilliant Hamilton had sabotaged his own career with an anti-Adams pamphlet, called 'an extended tantrum in print' by Hamilton biographer Ron Chernow.[10] The pamphlet attacked the president's character and Adams, who got 65 votes, blamed it for his defeat.

It's still unclear why Jefferson and Burr got the same number of votes, with their party seemingly failing to arrange for one of the votes not to go to Burr. The tie shoved the contingent election into the Federalist-controlled and Jefferson-hostile House of Representatives, which would decide the president from among the top five finishers, as laid out in the Constitution.

The House finally chose Jefferson on the 36th ballot with less than a month to Inauguration Day, helped by Burr-bashing Hamilton backing his usual opponent

Jefferson in what he saw as America's best interest. Burr became vice president.

For now it was crisis over after the first peaceful transition of power between political opponents. 'The constitutional miracle, if there was one, did not happen in the Philadelphia of 1787 but in the Washington of 1801,' wrote Bruce Akerman. 'It is one thing to write a Constitution; quite another for it to survive; and still another for it to survive in a world for which it was not designed.'[11] The mess led to the 12th Amendment being ratified in time for the 1804 election so that electors would in future have to cast separate votes for president and vice president.

Adams had become the first president to live at the White House in 1800 but Jefferson was the first president whose inauguration took place in Washington. Adams wasn't there on 4 March, having left Washington early on Inauguration Day despite still technically being president. If he had seen early riser Jefferson, who 'once claimed that he had not slept past sunrise in more than 50 years', he surely didn't wave.[12]

In his first inaugural address, the always charming Jefferson said, 'We are all Republicans, we are all Federalists.'[13]

1804 Election

It was so much simpler in 1804 as Jefferson romped home 162-14, including all three votes from 'Buckeye State' Ohio (17th, 1803), against Federalist opponent Charles Cotesworth Pinckney. George Clinton became Jefferson's vice president after beating Rufus King by exactly the same result in the first separate election for the No. 2 post.

Jefferson went into the election having orchestrated the Louisiana Purchase with France in 1803. The gigantic deal involved the U.S. acquiring 'approximately 827,000 square miles of land west of the Mississippi River for $15 million'.[14] Around 15 U.S. states, some in their entirety, derive from the bulk buy.

1808 Election

Pinckney remained politically perky as the Federalists recovered a bit of ground in the 1808 election. But they couldn't stop Jefferson, a 57-year-old Virginian at his first inauguration, being replaced by James Madison, another 57-year-old Virginian and also a Democratic-Republican.

Madison, America's shortest-ever president at 5'4", an inch smaller than size-conscious Leonard in *The Big Bang Theory*, won 122-47.[15] Amid some murmuring, Madison became the third Virginian in the country's first four presidents (Massachusetts-born Adams was the odd man out). James Monroe would later make this four in five.

In his first inaugural address, Madison praised his three predecessors amid the dawning realisation that the presidential club would be an exclusive one.

1812 Election

America had already declared war against Britain by the time of the 1812 election. Worryingly for the president, it was being labelled 'Mr Madison's War' by opponents. A low point of the conflict saw British troops burn down the White House in 1814. Sorry about that.

'Father of the Constitution' Madison faced 'Father of the Erie Canal' and New York City Mayor DeWitt Clinton, who was backed by the Federalists and some stroppy Democratic-Republicans.

Madison won 128-89, including three votes from 'Pelican State' Louisiana (18th, 1812), while Clinton got 29 votes from New York, which now had top spot in the Electoral College. It would stay there until ousted by California in 1972.

1816 Election

The war with Britain had defined Madison's second term. It's now known as the War of 1812, though it was officially ended by the Treaty of Ghent in Belgium on 24 December 1814. With communications slow – a key factor influencing the Electoral College debate a quarter of a century earlier at the Constitutional Convention – a major battle took place on 8 January 1815 at New Orleans, with Jackson in charge of the victorious American forces.

The war was a disaster for the Federalists, who appeared disloyal to many voters. The conflict would give America a national anthem as Francis Scott Key watched the British bombard Fort McHenry in Baltimore in 1814, producing the opening inquiry 'Oh, say can you see by the dawn's early light' with the Star-Spangled Banner still proudly waving 'O'er the land of the free and the home of the brave'.

Democratic-Republican Monroe thrashed final Federalist Rufus King 183-34. New kid on the block 'Hoosier State' Indiana (19th, 1816) backed Monroe.

1820 Election

Change was afoot in 1820. It was the last election before the majority of states let their electors be chosen by voters, rather than state legislatures, and that would require a different campaign style. 'Parades, barbecues, songs, and slogans became typical electioneering tools in the period of 1820–1852.'[16]

Monroe's time in office overlaps with what's known as 'The Era of Good Feelings' despite a major financial crash known as the Panic of 1819. The Missouri Compromise of 1820 was aimed at keeping a balance between free states and slave states. It defined where slavery could not go, as opposition to the slavery of the South grew in the North, and opposition to the North's opposition grew in the South. The Compromise bought time for the United States, and time was crucial with Lincoln only 11 years old.

The 1820 result was 231 votes for the unopposed Monroe and a single vote for future president John Quincy Adams. The faithless elector this time was New Hampshire's William Plumer. He backed JQA, who wasn't even running. Some say Plumer wanted Washington to always be the only unanimously elected president; others say he didn't like Monroe.

'Magnolia State' Mississippi (20th, 1817), 'Prairie State' Illinois (21st, 1818), 'Heart of Dixie' Alabama (22nd, 1819), 'Pine Tree State' Maine (23rd, 1820) and 'Show Me State' Missouri (24th, 1821) voted for the first time.

1824 Election

America was about to be tested again.

The 1800 election debacle had required the 12th Amendment so that no intended vice president could ever again pose a threat to his own presidential candidate. Displaying a sense of humour, the Electoral College moved from two winners in 1800 to no clear winner at all in

1824. The contest involved four Democratic-Republicans, making a majority much harder to get, after the breaking down of the 'King Caucus' system under which candidates were chosen by congressional big boys.

Jackson finished on 99 electoral votes; John Quincy Adams, son of President John Adams, received 84; William H. Crawford won 41; and Henry Clay came out with 37.

Since nobody had a majority, the House of Representatives had to decide among the top three candidates in another contingent election. House Speaker Clay fell victim to the 12th Amendment, which had changed it from top five in the original Constitution. Clay backed Adams and was later made Secretary of State in what a furious Jackson denounced as a 'corrupt bargain'.

The 24 states in the House of Representatives had one vote each, requiring agreement among themselves, and Adams was selected as president on the first ballot with 13 votes. Jackson, who topped the original popular and electoral vote, got only seven. The remaining four went to Crawford.

In his inaugural address, Adams didn't avoid the controversy: 'Less possessed of your confidence in advance than any of my predecessors, I am deeply conscious of the prospect that I shall stand more and oftener in need of your indulgence.'

1828 Election

With 'defeat' festering in the Jackson camp for four long years, the 1828 election was always going to be brutal. In an unrestrained campaign, 'the backers of Adams, like Jackson's partisans, soon descended into the gutter', accusing Jackson of 'adultery, gambling, cock fighting, bigamy, slave-trading, drunkenness, theft, lying, and murder'.[17]

Jackson's beloved wife, Rachel Donelson Jackson, died shortly after the campaign finished in December 1828. Jackson blamed her death on all the abuse, particularly the bigamy comments. He and Rachel had married without realising at the time that her divorce had not come through. They quickly fixed this by remarrying in 1794. Friends of the couple were no doubt careful over the exact phrasing on their wedding cards.

As for murder, Jackson had approved the execution of six militiamen for desertion in wartime in 1813. His opponents distributed the infamous 'Coffin Handbill' during the 1828 election showing six coffins and disputing the charges of desertion.

One consequence of the excessive mudslinging was that 'nothing at all was said about what the candidates would do if elected'.[18]

Populist and popular, Jackson won 178-83, with National Republican candidate Adams remaining strong in New England.

In his first inaugural address, Jackson, a firm believer in people power but also a slave owner, declared that government must be 'administered for the good of the people' and 'regulated by their will'.

Raucous inaugural celebrations inside the White House among Jackson's supporters meant carpets 'smelled of cheese for months after the party'. The mob was enticed out of the building by servants setting up 'washtubs full of juice and whiskey on the White House lawn'.[19]

1832 Election

National party conventions were held for the first time in 1832, with their most exciting function the choice of presidential candidate.

The Democratic Party, as it now was, saw Jackson beat National Republican Clay 219-49. The Second Bank of the United States dominated the campaign, or at least Jackson's veto of its re-charter did. The mostly single-issue election offered a lesson to future candidates: one issue is enough to win as long as it's the right one.

Jackson dealt firmly with the 1832–33 Nullification Crisis after South Carolina threatened to ignore a federal tariff. It was a foretaste of much worse trouble to come, and Lincoln was now in his mid-20s.

Jackson would turn out to be the last two-term president until Lincoln, deep into the Civil War.

1836 Election

In January 1835, there was the first known assassination attempt on a president when Richard Lawrence, a mentally ill house painter born in England, had misfires from separate pistols as Jackson came out of a Washington funeral service in the Capitol Building itself. Of the two men, Lawrence probably came closer to death that day as Jackson, 'enraged by the event, struggled to get at him with his cane'.[20]

For the 1836 election, opponents borrowed from English political parlance to rally round the Whig banner in sarcastic opposition to 'King Andrew' but there were still more fans than enemies and Jackson's vice president, Martin Van Buren, won with 170 votes. Among the three Whig rivals running in an apparent display of party indiscipline, William Henry Harrison was top with 73. Time to start writing that speech WHH!

Van Buren received the votes of 'Natural State/Land of Opportunity' Arkansas (25th, 1836) and 'Great Lakes State/Wolverine State' Michigan (26th, 1837).

A skilled political operator known as the 'Little Magician', Van Buren was the first president born after the Declaration of Independence.

The 1836 election was the only time so far that the Senate has decided who will be the vice president. Unlike one vote for every state in the House of Representatives, all senators have a vote each in choosing between the top two finishers, not three, in the Electoral College. Van Buren's running mate Richard M. Johnson finished one electoral vote short of a majority before winning 33-16 against Francis Granger in the Senate vote.

1840 Election

Another financial crisis, the Panic of 1837, set up the Whigs for their first successful assault on the presidency, this time involving a direct face-off between Van Buren and Harrison.

Harrison's campaign turned insults to their advantage, in particular a jibe over the 67-year-old Harrison spending his days drinking hard cider in a log cabin. That led to huge rallies involving log cabins and indeed hard cider.

'Old Tippecanoe', a nickname earned from a military victory, easily beat Van Buren 234-60 and proceeded on 4 March 1841 to give what remains the longest-ever inaugural address at 1 hour, 45 minutes in freezing weather. No interjections of 'Wrap it up mate' were recorded during the speech of 8,445 words, almost 63 times as long as Washington's address in 1792.

Washington's 135 words include 'Fellow Citizens' at the start. Harrison's total (some say it's 8,444, but nobody wants to re-read it) includes, 'The first Roman Emperor, in his attempt to seize the sacred treasure, silenced the opposition of the officer to whose charge it had been committed by a significant allusion to his sword.'

It has been suggested the address was so long because Harrison was keen to show he was no fool. If that's true, it's a genuinely tragic presidency with his dreams vanishing as he went down with pneumonia weeks later.[21] Harrison died 31 days after his extended soliloquy.

History has not been kind to Harrison and his spell in office, the shortest presidency of all time. Trend's 'Presidents of the United States' flash cards have a 'Noteworthy Events' section. For Lincoln, it's gigantic landmarks in American history such as 'Served as president during the Civil War' and 'Emancipation Proclamation, freeing slaves in the states that had left the Union'.

Harrison's sole entry is 'Steam fire engine publicly tested in New York'.

1844 Election

In 1840 John Tyler was part of the Whig campaign slogan: 'Tippecanoe and Tyler too.' Now for the first time, an incumbent president had died: 1789–1841 is the second-longest period in American history without a presidential death in office, trailing only JFK's death in 1963 to the present day.

Tyler set an important precedent by assuming the presidency as a full president rather than as a vice president becoming an acting president before another election. At that stage the 'correct' procedure was unclear.

Tyler was the father of 15 children, a presidential record, from marriages to Letitia Christian and Julia Gardiner. A big family can be expensive, and 'the necessity of having to sell a favourite house slave, Ann Eliza, to raise cash to move to Washington in 1827 was a sad experience for Tyler'.[22]

Mockingly called 'His Accidency' by his many critics, Tyler didn't run again in the 1844 election and Clay fancied another go.

The Democrats went for Tennessee's James K. Polk, a 'dark-horse' candidate chosen by his party on the ninth ballot. Knox, not Kevin, in case you're wondering.

One future state dominated the election. Polk backed the annexation of Texas – despite political concerns over slavery expanding as America grew – and beat Clay 170-105. The popular vote was far closer, with Clay only 39,000 votes behind in his third presidential defeat. James Birney ran for the new anti-slavery Liberty Party, getting 2.3 per cent of the popular vote.

Clay had stumbled by opposing annexation of then independent Texas, which had formerly been part of Mexico but wished to join with the U.S., which it finally did at the end of 1845. The U.S. and Mexico went to war from 1846 to 1848, with the Americans easily coming out on top and winning an even bigger prize than Texas: California.

1848 Election

Polk was a hard-working president who had pledged in advance to serve only one term. Thoroughly knackered, he died three months after leaving office in 1849 at age 53.

The Whigs went back to choosing a general in 1848, the first time the country had the same Election Day. Zachary Taylor came through for them by beating Lewis Cass 163-127 amid talk of 'manifest destiny' for America to expand.

Amongst the newcomers, 'Sunshine State' Florida (27th, 1845) backed Taylor. 'Lone Star State' Texas (28th, 1845) supported Cass, who also won 'Hawkeye State' Iowa (29th, 1846) and 'Badger State' Wisconsin (30th, 1848).

Former president Van Buren ran for the anti-slavery Free-Soil Party, attracting 10 per cent of the popular vote nationally, and may have cost Cass the presidency.

And then another shock.

Even Columbo would have struggled with reports of Taylor's 'Death by Cherries' with lashings of cold milk on a very hot 1850 day after attending a Washington Monument ceremony on Independence Day. Severe gastro-intestinal problems followed and he died on 9 July.

Millard Fillmore was the new president, ineffectual, pro-South and the wrong man at the wrong time. America was having too many of these presidents as Civil War loomed.

1852 Election

The Whigs went for another general, Winfield Scott, on the 53rd ballot. The Democrats were far more decisive, selecting New Hampshire's Franklin Pierce on the 49th ballot.

The Compromise of 1850, which admitted 'Golden State' California (31st, 1850) as a free state, also brought in the Fugitive Slave Act whereby escaped slaves were controversially returned to their legal owners. The nation's divisions were growing, and Lincoln was now in his 40s.

Pierce easily won 254-42. Not only did the Whigs lose but they were ominously disappearing from the South.

For Pierce, the lead-up to his presidency was dominated by tragedy when he lost his 11-year-old son Benjamin in a gruesome train accident in January 1853.[23]

1856 Election

Now often seen as the party of big business and low taxes, it's often forgotten that the first issue on which the newly born Republican Party fought a presidential election was the extension of slavery (which it opposed). Supporters of the party focused on the North in 1856, which made sense because they would have been beaten senseless in the South.

The first-ever Republican Party candidate, explorer John C. Fremont, wasn't expected to win and didn't. Democratic candidate James Buchanan, who had already held major posts in government, became the next president with a 174-114 victory. However, Fremont did well enough under the slogan 'Free Soil, Free Speech, Fremont' or variants thereof to suggest 1860 would be considerably closer.

'The Pathfinder' was maybe looking for new excitement. He had finished a final expedition which 'lacked the grisly drama of some of the previous four. No one ate anyone else, although at one point of low rations Fremont swore everyone to abstinence from human flesh and vowed to shoot the first man who eyed his fellow hungrily.'[24]

Former president Fillmore headed the anti-immigrant American Party or Know-Nothings (going back to the time when supporters would reply they knew nothing when asked about their organisation) and got eight electoral votes despite giving the Democrats some competition in the South.

It was a dreadful time for all Americans, with war seemingly drawing closer every year and politicians powerless to stop it. 'The combustible mixture of Northern abolitionism, Southern slavery and Western expansion ignited the fuse of secession that exploded into Civil War,' Roper wrote. 'Faced with the impossibility of reconciling sectional differences, Buchanan did little to postpone what he and many of his contemporaries considered inevitable: the break-up of the United States.'[25]

The country had already taken a body blow from the disastrous 1854 Kansas–Nebraska Act, strongly backed by 'Little Giant' Stephen A. Douglas. This overturned several barrels of worms by overturning the Missouri Compromise, which restricted where slavery could go. It allowed 'popular sovereignty' in territories to decide whether they would eventually be free or slave states, triggering what became known as 'Bleeding Kansas'. This was 'a bloody struggle, with much loss of life, between free-soilers and pro-slavery settlers for control of Kansas'.[26]

1860 Election

Shortly after the swearing-in of Buchanan, the only bachelor president so far, the Supreme Court's Dred Scott case ruled 7-2 against a legal bid for freedom by a slave, Dred Scott, after he had lived in a free state. The ruling also declared the Missouri Compromise to be unconstitutional and, in its most shameful decision, the court claimed basic rights didn't apply to African Americans. Contrast with Lincoln who declared in a letter, admittedly as late as 1864, 'If slavery is not wrong, nothing is wrong.'

And everything was going wrong. Ahead of the 1860 election, the Democratic Party – America's political glue – was coming apart, with different candidates serving different regions and different interests. They were big interests. By 1857 Stampp says southern slavery was 'an entrenched and flourishing institution, providing most of the labour for the production of the South's staple crops. Nearly 400,000 masters had a capital investment of $2 billion in nearly 4,000,000 slaves distributed over 15 southern states.'[27]

The Democrats were clearly split – John C. Breckinridge stood for the southern faction and got 72 electoral votes in the South, and Douglas, who campaigned around the country, got just 12 electoral votes, which serves him right. Constitutional Union candidate John Bell pleaded for conciliation. He got 39.

That left only the Republican Party candidate, and it was the man who would end up in 'the hearts of the people for whom he saved the Union' as the Lincoln Memorial puts it. No references to the game of darts can be found anywhere in his correspondence but Lincoln won with 180 and was supported by new states 'North Star State' Minnesota (32nd, 1858) and 'Beaver State' Oregon (33rd, 1859). His election proved too much for seven southern states, led by South Carolina, who had already left the Union in defence of its 'peculiar institution' by the time of Lincoln's inaugural address.

Lincoln was conciliatory in that speech: 'One section of our country believes slavery is right and ought to be extended, while the other believes it is wrong and ought not to be extended. This is the only substantial dispute.' He finished with a stirring plea to opponents to remember the past: 'We are not enemies, but friends … The mystic chords of memory, stretching from every battlefield and patriot grave to every living heart and hearthstone all over this broad land, will yet swell the chorus of the Union, when again touched, as surely they will be, by the better angels of our nature.'

1864 Election

Like many humorous people, President Lincoln had a pessimistic side though sometimes it was hard to tell if he was being serious. The jury's still out on his wedding day comment (4 November 1842, to Mary Todd). Dressed smartly and asked by a friend where he was going, Lincoln replied: 'To hell, I reckon.'[28] The marriage wasn't pure happiness, but it lasted with genuine affection.

Lincoln feared he could still lose the 1864 election, which risked undoing all the achievements and sacrifices of the previous years, including the historic emancipation of slaves in Confederate states amid a bloody conflict which had claimed hundreds of thousands of lives.

He needn't have worried. Democratic candidate George B. McClellan was the cautious former commander of the Union forces (though popular with his troops) who had been afflicted with what Lincoln called the 'slows'. In a famous putdown, Lincoln reputedly wrote, 'If General McClellan does not want to use the army, I would like to borrow it for a time.'

McClellan was wiped out by electoral forces loyal to Lincoln, including soldiers, in the remaining Union states taking part in the election. 'Sunflower State' Kansas (34th, 1861), 'Mountain State' West Virginia (35th, 1863) and 'Silver State' Nevada (36th, 1864) all backed Lincoln in the 212-21 win, with McClellan only getting votes from Delaware, border state Kentucky and New Jersey.

Lincoln appeared calm on Election Night, which was 'rainy and foggy in Washington, and the President spent the evening at the War Department waiting for the returns. The first reports were encouraging, and he sent them over to Mrs. Lincoln, saying, "She is more anxious than I."'[29]

Lincoln's second inaugural address mixed forceful imagery ('until every drop of blood drawn with the lash shall be paid by another drawn with the sword') with typical eloquence: 'With malice toward none, with charity for all, with firmness in the right as God gives us to see the right, let us strive on to finish the work we are in, to bind up the nation's wounds.'

This book praises Lincoln throughout, but he was far from perfect. In 1858, Lincoln said he was not in favour of 'the social and political equality of the white and black races' and there was even worse. Fans will put such comments down to the overwhelming racism of the society in which he spoke, such as that comment in a series of famous debates against Douglas. Others will argue he meant it.

Whatever you think of the great man, one thing is clear: Lincoln was not intending to get his revenge on the South. But he was soon to pay a huge personal sacrifice of his own.

6

The Drinker to the Thinker
1868–1944

America had grown from 13 states in 1790 to 37 in 1870, and its population from just under four million to more than 38 million.

This chapter starts with Civil War warrior-turned-president Ulysses S. Grant who, like Harry S. Truman, had to explain what the 'S' in his name stood for.[1] It ends with Truman's boss, Franklin Delano Roosevelt, the only three-time and four-time president.

FDR utilised professors to back his cause and had a brains trust, but he's mostly called a 'thinker' here because it rhymes with 'drinker', which Grant definitely was, though not to the extent it interfered with his military or political command. Abraham Lincoln joked he wanted whatever Grant was drinking to be given to his other generals.

Lincoln, America's greatest president, was shot on Good Friday 14 March 1865, while watching a comedy called *Our American Cousin*. His assassin, the actor and southern sympathiser John Wilkes Booth, used the expected laughter at 'you sockdologizing old man-trap' to shoot the 56-year-old president in the back of the head while he was at Ford's Theater in D.C. Barely a week earlier, the South had surrendered at Appomattox Court House.

1868 Election

Andrew Johnson had replaced Hannibal Hamlin as Lincoln's vice president and caused deep offence by being drunk at the 1865 inauguration as he 'babbled on incoherently, delivering a tirade of self-serving remarks and alienating nearly the entire cabinet'.[2] Addressing individuals directly, at one point Johnson had to stop and ask for the name of the Secretary of the Navy.

Johnson was drafted onto the ticket as a politically helpful loyal southerner and was sworn in as president when Lincoln was assassinated. Johnson never got to deliver a presidential inaugural address, for which tickets would have sold very well.

Distrusted from the start, Johnson narrowly survived conviction in the Senate after being impeached in the House of Representatives by Radical Republicans angry at his moderate stance towards the defeated South.

Grant won the 1868 election against Democratic candidate Horatio Seymour 214-80 and got the support of 'Cornhusker State' Nebraska (37th, 1867).

1872 Election

Horace Greeley for the Democrats died before November was out and his votes were redistributed. It didn't matter as Grant had won convincingly.

Grant 'won re-election by a decisive 55 per cent of the vote' and 286 electoral votes, with 63 of Greeley's votes given to other candidates.[3]

Lincoln in 1864 also got 55 per cent but Grant's decimal point was bigger than Lincoln's: 55.6 to 55.1.

1876 Election

The 1876 election is a landmark for the Electoral College as the man who got a quarter of a million more popular votes lost the electoral vote and the presidency. Unlike Jackson in 1824, Democratic candidate Samuel J. Tilden actually had a majority, gaining 51 per cent against Rutherford B. Hayes.

Grant may have been tempted to go for a controversial third term but the Panic of 1873 and corruption scandals in his administration ended any hope of that.

Instead, 100 years on from the Declaration of Independence, 'Centennial State' Colorado (38th, 1876) backed Hayes in the year where every vote counted.

Held barely a decade since the Civil War ended, a standoff between the two major parties grew increasingly tense as Inauguration Day approached.

Hayes finally won 185-184 but gained the unwanted nickname 'His Fraudulency' and 'Rutherfraud'. He wisely said he would be a one-term president.

What happened? 'The 1876 election remains infamous for the fraud and vote stealing on both sides and the controversial awarding of 20 disputed electoral votes from Florida, Louisiana, South Carolina, and Oregon' to Hayes.[4] A 15-man Electoral Commission set up to look at the disputes, including rival states' multiple submissions which had different winners, consistently went Hayes' way.

Two days before inauguration, the parties came to an agreement whereby Hayes would be president but the price of that deal saw Reconstruction – making sure the South respected civil rights – tragically tossed aside for another 90 years.

1880 Election

The 1880 election was much closer than 1876 in popular votes, with the 214-155 electoral vote winner and next president James A. Garfield getting 48.3 per cent of the vote to Winfield S. Hancock's 48.2 per cent, and winning by less than 10,000 votes. As consolation, Hancock always knew his middle name was Scott.

Garfield struggled to finish writing his inaugural address on time. 'As the day approached, he had an anxiety dream in which he fell off a canal boat and was suddenly standing naked in the wilderness during a wild storm.'[5] Important: Any future presidential candidate who has this exact dream should mention it to the Secret Service.

Garfield was shot on 2 July 1881 at a Washington train station by Charles Guiteau before going on to die from his wounds 79 days later. Guiteau reputedly had the nerve to claim 'the doctors killed Garfield, I just shot him'. Guiteau was probably right in his claim of medical negligence, with endless click-and-collect visits by the president's bullet-seeking doctors.

To recap, Garfield fell off a canal boat and was inaugurated in March, got shot in July and died in September.

1884 Election

Despite scandalous though possibly true accusations of being the father of an 'illegitimate' child, Grover Cleveland became the first Democrat elected since the Civil War.

Four words sank the very popular James Blaine's campaign for president and the Republican didn't say any of them.

Arise Revd Samuel D. Burchard, chosen to speak at an event organised in New York. Assuring Blaine he was among Republicans, Burchard said, '(We) don't propose to leave our party and identify ourselves with the party whose antecedents have been *rum, Romanism and rebellion*.'[6]

In what had been a vitriolic campaign to start with, the minister's triple insult saw Cleveland take the 36 electoral votes of New York and beat Blaine – often known as 'The Plumed Knight', but we don't need to get into that right now – 219-182. New York's vote determined the winner. Cleveland won the state by around 1,000 votes – or 500 offended Catholics.

The 1884 election also gave us the template for what potential candidates who really don't want to run have to say. General William Tecumseh Sherman, wanted by the Republicans, stated: 'If drafted, I will not run. If nominated, I will not accept. If elected, I will not serve'. Congressman Mo Udall of Arizona is credited with 'If nominated, I will run to Mexico. If elected, I will fight extradition.'[7]

1888 Election

In their first of two meetings, largely fought over tariffs, Benjamin Harrison beat Cleveland 233-168 despite losing the popular vote by around 100,000 with a turnout of just under 80 per cent.

'Harrison carried Indiana by a margin of 0.4 per cent and New York by 1.1 per cent. These were the only states to shift from Cleveland's 1884 list, but they were enough to put Harrison ahead in the electoral college.'[8] Revd Burchard was not invited by the Harrison camp to say grace in either of these states.

The dignified Cleveland left his 75-year-old vice presidential candidate Allen Thurman to campaign 'but he often digressed to mention his personal ailments'.[9]

1892 Election

For the Harrison–Cleveland rematch, the number of states jumped from 38 to 44, although between them the extra six states only had 20 votes, still less than Ohio on 23.

The states voting for the first time included 'Peace Garden State' North Dakota (39th, 1889) and 'Mount Rushmore State' South Dakota (40th, 1889). Other new voters were 'Treasure State' Montana (41st, 1889), 'Evergreen State' Washington (42nd, 1889), 'Gem State' Idaho (43rd, 1890) and 'Equality State' Wyoming (44th, 1890).

Cleveland won his third popular vote in a row and also triumphed in the Electoral College 277-145.

1896 Election

Silver had shimmered and simmered for years and this was its time on the big stage, with farmers and progressives part of the cause. 'Free coinage meant that the mints would coin all the silver offered to them', and supporters believed 'silver meant prosperity. Added to the currency, it would swell the money stock and quicken the pace of economic activity.'[10]

Despite Bryan's impassioned speech at the 1896 Democratic convention, in which he warned, 'You shall not crucify mankind on a cross of gold', it would be the first of three losses for the 36-year-old 'Boy Orator'. William McKinley, once accused of having 'no more backbone than a chocolate éclair', won 271-176. 'Beehive State' Utah (45th, 1896) overwhelmingly went for Bryan.

It was a significant result. 'The Republicans became the party of the cities, of workers and industrialists ... The only two presidential elections that the Republicans lost over the next nine (including 1896) were those won by Woodrow Wilson', involving a split opposition in 1912 and a narrow win in 1916.[11]

1900 Election

Theodore Roosevelt was causing trouble in New York, so his local party helped to arrange for him to disappear by becoming vice president. That tactic backfired somewhat when fourth child Leon Czolgosz shot McKinley while the president 'stood greeting a line of well-wishers at the Pan-American Exposition in Buffalo, New York' on 6 September 1901.[12]

McKinley had already done the hard work for Roosevelt by winning re-election in 1900, beating Bryan 292-155, after the Spanish–American War of 1898, which saw the U.S. expand overseas with its territories including the Philippines, Guam and Puerto Rico.

The 42-year-old Roosevelt remains the youngest president. Kennedy is the youngest elected present at 43.

1904 Election

Amid continued industrial unrest and huge social inequality, America had been having a taste of TR's 'Square Deal', which, according to one biographer, was where 'the rich man should have justice, and that the poor man should have justice, and that no man should have more or less'.[13]

Trust-buster Theodore Roosevelt, popular for progressive reforms and making a name for himself as the first president deeply concerned about the environment, beat Democratic opponent Alton B. Parker 336-140 and with a majority of more than 2.5 million.

1908 Election

Theodore Roosevelt respected the two-term tradition, and William H. Taft ended Bryan's third attempt at the presidency with a 321-162 win. 'Sooner State' Oklahoma (46th, 1907) went for Bryan.

The heaviest president at around 330 pounds, or more than 23 stone, one famous anecdote had the jovial Taft mentioning he had been for a horse ride, triggering a telegram in response which asked, 'How is the horse?'

1912 Election

Teddy Roosevelt was back despite being shot in October 1912 in Milwaukee by John Schrank, a troubled individual like so many would-be assassins. Roosevelt went ahead with a speech before getting looked at by doctors, with a bullet in the ribs near the heart.

Representing the Progressives, the Bull Moose nickname for his party came about in 1912 after Roosevelt, a keen environmentalist (and hunter), was asked 'a simple question about how his health and spirits were holding up. "I'm feeling like a bull moose!" Roosevelt said. This image – of a huge antlered member of the biggest deer family – became the symbol of Roosevelt's campaign.'[14]

'Land of Enchantment' New Mexico (47th, 1912) and 'Grand Canyon State' Arizona (48th, 1912) both supported Democratic candidate Woodrow Wilson, and the numbers were always against Taft.

Wilson beat Roosevelt 435-88. Taft got just eight votes, from Utah and Vermont.

1916 Election

The First World War was in its third year by the time of the presidential election, and Wilson campaigned on the powerful slogan 'He kept us out of war'. There was no third term in 1920 to test out the corollary: 'He did not keep us out of war'.

In his Shadow Lawn speech, Wilson had gone as far as claiming, 'If you elect my opponent, you elect a war.'[15] That opponent was Republican Charles Evans Hughes, a former Justice of the Supreme Court and a future Chief Justice. The result was very close, 277-254, with California's 13 electoral votes proving the crucial difference.

Wilson won in November, was sworn in for a second time in March 1917, and America entered the war in April.

1920 Election

Wilson suffered a serious stroke in 1919. His frailty thereafter was largely hidden from Congress and the press, with work widely believed to have gone through his wife Edith.

Republican Warren Harding easily beat James Cox 404-127 in the election, with women voting for the first time under the 19th Amendment.

1924 Election

Harding ran a corrupt administration and died in office in 1923.

Vice President Calvin Coolidge, famous as 'Silent Cal' for not saying much, took over, did not say much and beat John W. Davis 382-136.

1928 Election

New York Governor Al Smith became the first Catholic to run for president with a major party, in his case for the Democrats.

The 'Happy Warrior' also has dinners in his honour where presidential candidates in an election year are meant to temporarily switch off from politics and give light-hearted speeches mostly making fun of themselves. Trump's speech in 2016 was particularly memorable for the audacity of its jibes against Hillary Clinton, including, 'Here she is tonight, in public, pretending not to hate Catholics', which drew jeers.

The 1928 race wasn't the purest of elections: 'Unfortunately, one issue of the campaign – that of Smith's Catholicism – hung over the election process in ways that would reflect badly on the Republican side for decades.'[16] As Goldwater helped to ideologically pave the way for Reagan in 1980, Smith did likewise in the world of religion for Kennedy in 1960.

Republican candidate Herbert Hoover won 444-87. In his only inaugural address, Hoover, a Quaker, chastised the nation over the ongoing prohibition: 'There would be little traffic in illegal liquor if only criminals patronized it.'[17]

1932 Election

Amid mass unemployment and a country caught in the headlights of the Great Depression, FDR won a landslide victory, beating Hoover 472-59.

The win ushered in the New Deal of big public works and an active interventionist role for the government.

Roosevelt went on to give one of the greatest inaugural addresses, telling America, 'This great nation will endure as it has endured, will revive and will prosper. So, first of all, let me assert my firm belief that the only thing we have to fear is fear itself – nameless, unreasoning, unjustified terror which paralyzes needed efforts to convert retreat into advance.'

1936 Election

In 1936, FDR annihilated Alf Landon 523-8, with the unfortunate Republican winning only Maine and Vermont.

This is the all-time biggest win for contested elections in terms of Electoral College vote percentages.

Maybe Landon wasn't so unlucky, as he went on to become the first Democratic or Republican presidential candidate to live to 100. President Reagan celebrated the approaching centenary with Landon in Kansas in 1987 and remarked, 'You don't know what a joy it is for a fellow like me to go to a birthday party for someone who can in all honesty call me kid.'[18]

1940 Election

It took him a long time to announce but FDR daringly broke the two-term tradition, deciding that the international circumstances justified what was still seen then as a shocking move. It didn't affect his electoral invincibility as he beat Wendell Willkie 449-82, and the U.S. would enter the global conflict at the end of 1941.

Did FDR know he was heading for the presidential pantheon by this stage? In his inaugural address he said, 'In Washington's day the task of the people was to create and weld together a nation. In Lincoln's day the task of the people was to preserve that nation from disruption from within. In this day the task of the people is to save that nation and its institutions from disruption from without.'

1944 Election

FDR was superb at winding up Republicans and responded to their criticism of him chasing a fourth term with 'The first 12 years are the hardest'.[19]

FDR was a passionate forester at his family estate, Hyde Park. One observer of the 1944 election said about Election Day: 'At the Town Hall the President gave his occupation as "tree grower" and was given the 251st ballot.'[20]

Roosevelt beat Thomas Dewey 432-99.

In his inaugural address, FDR said, 'We have learned that we must live as men, not as ostriches, nor as dogs in the manger. We have learned to be citizens of the world, members of the human community.'

7

When Harry Met Dewey to Enter the Donald

1948–2016

Even in the 21st century, the United States hasn't long put the Civil War safely away in its history books. Gertrude Janeway, the last widow of a Union soldier to have fought in the great conflict, died in 2003 after getting married at age 18 to John Janeway in 1927.[1]

The South won this last battle, with Alberta Martin dying at age 97 in 2004. She had married a Confederate veteran, William Martin, in 1927 when she was 21. There were age gaps and Civil War pensions for both marriages.

The period covered in this chapter includes another searing event in the country's history – the atrocities of 11 September 2001. It starts with the 33rd president, Harry Truman, and ends with Donald Trump's shock win in 2016.

By 1950 the United States had a population of 150 million and 48 states, with only Alaska and Hawaii still to join in 1959. The nation had emerged from another conflict, the

Second World War, as an active global superpower with a nuclear arsenal.

1948 Election

Harry 'Give 'Em Hell' Truman was not known for his shyness. As far forward as 1960, Democratic candidate John F. Kennedy was having to defend Truman's choice of words in telling Republicans to 'go to hell'.

Truman had become president after the death of Franklin Delano Roosevelt on 12 April 1945. Visibly exhausted and very ill, FDR died at his own 'Little White House' retreat in Georgia, triggering nationwide mourning. He had been president since 1933 and was still only 63. Against many people's expectations, Truman proved an efficient leader, and one prepared to take enormous decisions, none bigger than the terrible atomic bombing – twice – of Japan.

For the 1948 election, which he was expected to lose, Truman criticised the 'Do Nothing' 80th Congress and called it back into session to enact the Republican platform of policy agreed at the national convention. He also got on a train and started a 'Whistle Stop' tour which proved extremely popular. 'It was estimated that three million people saw him on his two-week trip through 18 states', and at one stop 'he appeared in bathrobe and pajamas'.[2]

People nonetheless thought Truman would lose against Republican challenger Thomas Dewey, and the most famous photo in politics remains the president gleefully holding up the *Chicago Daily Tribune* front page boldly declaring DEWEY DEFEATS TRUMAN.

Truman won 303-189.

1952 Election

Truman still had much work to do on toning down his direct approach, gaining headlines in 1950 for threatening *Washington Post* music critic Paul Hume, who had criticised his daughter Margaret Truman's singing recital. Truman said in a letter that if they ever met Hume would need 'a new nose, a lot of beefsteak for black eyes, and perhaps a supporter below'!

Truman decided not to run in the 1952 election, battered by a troublesome Korean War, especially its commanders on the American side, and 'red scares' cropping up everywhere.

General Eisenhower, who had been Supreme Commander of almost everything in the Second World War, could probably have had either main party's nomination. He chose the Republicans and 'had a formula for victory – K1C2 (Korea, Communism, and corruption)'.[3] Others add Crime to the Cs. With television starting to play a major role, a campaign ad by Disney, 'I like Ike', featuring a happy elephant, worked wonders.

Eisenhower romped home by beating Democratic contender Adlai Stevenson 442-89. His vice president, Richard Nixon, needed the 'Checkers speech' during the campaign to survive revelations of secret funding from wealthy backers. Nixon went on TV and mentioned a gift he had accepted, but he wasn't going to upset the kids by taking away their black-and-white cocker spaniel called Checkers. The public loved it and Nixon was safe.

In his inaugural address, Ike said, 'We sense with all our faculties that forces of good and evil are massed and armed and opposed as rarely before in history.'

1956 Election

America was changing again, like it always does. A more decent Supreme Court, led by former California Governor Earl Warren, desegregated schools with its 1954 Brown vs. Board of Education of Topeka ruling.

Less seriously, and despite its prim reputation, the witty 50s saw the inimitable Phil Silvers playing the TV comedy role of Sergeant Bilko, a well-meaning army rascal who would get up at 'the crack of noon'.

Eisenhower was said to be a big Bilko fan. As for his presidential election, that was a repeat show as Ike thrashed Stevenson 457-73.

1960 Election

John F. Kennedy very narrowly won against Nixon, in the face of various tactics being employed to throw the election into the House of Representatives to make sure the South, still deeply segregated, got the best deal it could.

The first Catholic president won 303-219 in the electoral vote with 'Last Frontier State' Alaska (49th, 1959) backing Nixon and 'Aloha State' Hawaii (50th, 1959) supporting Kennedy.

Streetfighter Bobby Kennedy was campaign manager in 1960 for his older, taller, more accomplished and better-looking brother.[4]

JFK is not seen as a great president – he didn't have enough time, for starters – but his inaugural address is near the top: 'Let the word go forth from this time and place, to friend and foe alike, that the torch has been passed to a new generation of Americans.' The most famous part was: 'And so, my fellow Americans: ask not what your country can do for you – ask what you can do for your country.'

1964 Election

Kennedy was a wit, no other word for it. As a senator running for president he was asked at a press conference if he had been given a promised military intelligence briefing. JFK said yes and that he had talked to the Defense Department's General Wheeler. 'Question: What was his first name? Mr Kennedy: He didn't brief me on that.'[5]

JFK occasionally met other wits who had risen to the top of the political ladder. He shared his annoyance with British Prime Minister Harold Macmillan about press coverage of First Lady Jackie Kennedy. JFK is said to have asked Macmillan how he would react if somebody called his wife Dorothy a drunk. Macmillan allegedly replied: 'I would have said, "You should have seen her mother."'

But with Kennedy assassinated, and Vice President Lyndon B. Johnson now in the White House, the 1964 election campaign went back to the bad old mud-slinging days. Republican candidate Barry Goldwater was in no mood for moderation, famously declaring that 'extremism in the defence of liberty is no vice' and exhorting, 'Let's lob one into the men's room at the Kremlin.'

It was always very dangerous to bring up the subject of bodily functions with LBJ, who routinely dictated while sitting on the toilet. Many places, especially his ranch in Texas, seemed to bring out the worst in Johnson, who would startle visitors by suddenly taking a leak.

The Johnson camp's TV campaign spots against Goldwater included the most famous political TV attack ad, 'Daisy', which 'showed a little girl counting flower petals, counterposed against the countdown to a nuclear explosion'.[6]

LBJ crushed Goldwater with a record 61.1 per cent of the popular vote and 486-52 in electoral votes. Goldwater, with his solar-linked electronic flagpole, ran up home state Arizona and five southern states to form a pistol shape on the Electoral College map with the handle, Florida, backing LBJ.

The Electoral College for the first time totalled 538 votes. It has stayed at this number ever since.

1968 Election

Without the Vietnam War, LBJ would possibly be on Mount Rushmore. The massive achievements of his 'Great Society' programme include the 1964 Civil Rights Act and the Voting Rights Act of 1965, which would go a long way to ending what was in many states effectively an apartheid America. Landmark bills were passed in Medicare health insurance (elderly) and Medicaid (low-income).

All was overshadowed by the Vietnam War, where American families nervously watched draft numbers announced on TV in 1969 to see if their son, brother and husband would be drafted into a conflict that killed more than 58,000 Americans. Estimates of Vietnamese deaths and casualties range widely, but they're in the millions.

In the crazy year of 1968, LBJ announced on 31 March to considerable shock that he would not be running for president again. Robert F. Kennedy won the California Democratic primary shortly before being shot dead.

Nixon, running on law and order, won 301-191 against Hubert Humphrey, with segregationist George Wallace getting 46 electoral votes as the 'American Independent' candidate. Wallace's presence and performance helped both main candidates support a proposal to abolish the Electoral College; it gained support in the House of Representatives in 1969 but failed in the Senate.

1972 Election

Nixon made his 'Silent Majority' speech in November 1969, employing a phrase picked up by Trump in 2020, and destroyed Democratic opponent George McGovern 520-17 in the 1972 election.

Nixon's second inaugural address included a dig at JFK: 'In our own lives, let each of us ask – not just what will government do for me, but what can I do for myself?'

His presidency would explode thanks to the Watergate scandal, involving a break-in at Democratic headquarters at a Washington complex (called Watergate). The subsequent cover-up consumed the president. His vice president, Spiro Agnew, had already resigned over tax evasion. Ford took Agnew's place, on congressional approval, in 1973 and then the presidency itself in 1974 when Nixon resigned in the face of almost certain impeachment and, importantly, conviction in the Senate.

The Watergate break-in had been dismissed as a 'third-rate burglary' by Nixon's press secretary, and there seemed a lot of incompetence about in the 1970s, including one would-be bank robber. He failed spectacularly in Queens, New York, after the teller had 'collapsed on the floor laughing' upon reading a note 'demanding "your tens, twenties and thirties"'.[7]

1976 Election

Ford could take the jokes, mocking his own golf by saying a wayward shot would result in the warning shout 'FORD!' But his presidency never seriously recovered from his pardon for Nixon, and Carter skilfully portrayed himself as able to clean up Washington, a not unfamiliar theme in presidential elections.

A bid to abolish the Electoral College failed narrowly to pass in the Senate in 1979.

Carter won, but not easily. The end result was 297-240. His inaugural address got the tone just right: 'The American dream endures. We must once again have full faith in our country – and in one another.'

1980 Election

Carter never really stood a chance in 1980, with the economy struggling and American embassy hostages held in Iran (and released when Reagan became president).

Carter's 'Crisis of confidence' speech on 15 July 1979, not so different from his inaugural address, only made matters worse, with most Americans lacking confidence in him rather than themselves.

Reagan romped home 489-49.

In his inaugural address, Reagan was blunt: 'All of us need to be reminded that the Federal Government did not create the States; the States created the Federal Government.'

1984 Election

In Kansas, on a visit to Alf Landon to celebrate his 100th birthday in 1987, Reagan was in full flow: '(America) means a bright Kansas sun rising over fields that hardworking, broad-shouldered farmers have planted with prayers and ploughed with hope.'

For the election itself, Democratic candidate Walter Mondale was totally ploughed. Reagan won by around 17 million votes, in electoral terms 525-13, with Mondale winning home state Minnesota and D.C.

Geraldine Ferraro was Mondale's running mate, the first woman to get on a major party national ticket. Her *New York Times* obituary declared 'She Ended the Men's Club of National Politics'.

Plagued especially by the Iran–Contra affair, Reagan was nonetheless politically untouchable, becoming known as the 'Teflon President'. Often accused of laziness, again the opposite of Carter, one report said that 'the President has spent about one year of his 6½ years in office vacationing in California'.[8]

That brought to mind Reagan's oft-quoted joke: 'It's true that hard work never killed anybody, but I figure why take the chance.'[9]

1988 Election

Senator Gary Hart hit self-destruct on his campaign after telling the media they would be very bored if they staked him out. There followed allegations of adultery, a yacht called *Monkey Business* and 'a part-time actress named Donna Rice, 29, whose half-clad modelling photos soon graced newsstands across the country'.[10]

Hart was leading the 1988 race to take on George H. W. Bush. Without him the Democrats had the 'Seven Dwarfs', one of whom was Joe Biden. Massachusetts Governor Michael Dukakis eventually prevailed.

In a brutal campaign marred by racial overtones, Dukakis was battered by accusations he had released convicted murderer Willie Horton on furlough in Massachusetts, and that Horton had raped a woman while out of jail. A 'Revolving Door' attack ad showed prisoners going in and coming out of prison.

The debates finished Dukakis. CNN's Bernie Shaw opened the last of two debates by asking, 'If Kitty Dukakis were raped and murdered, would you favour an irrevocable death penalty for the killer?' The man called 'the Duke' should have vowed to hunt down and blast his wife's killer to death with a Smith & Wesson 500 before distributing body parts across key Electoral College states. Instead, to his personal credit, he said he had 'opposed the death penalty during all of my life' and 'there are better and more effective ways to deal with violent crime'.

Not even America has enough serial killers in important electoral states to make Dukakis' response politically profitable. His campaign had taken a fatal hit.

Broccoli-hating George H. W. Bush became the first sitting vice president to win the presidency since Martin Van Buren back in 1836 with a 426-111 win.[11]

1992 Election

Bill Clinton appeared to learn from Dukakis' ordeal, including the time the Arkansas governor was reported to have broken off campaigning in the New Hampshire primary to go back home for the 1992 execution of Rickey Ray Rector, who had killed Police Officer Robert Martin. At this stage, Rector was a brain-damaged man. With no clemency on offer from Clinton, 'at his last meal, he (Rector) saved the pecan pie as if he would be having it later'.[12]

Clinton gained from Texas billionaire Ross Perot doing particular damage to incumbent President George H. W. Bush. In response to suggestions in a debate that he lacked experience, Perot cuttingly admitted, 'I don't have any experience in running up a $4 trillion debt.'

Other memorable debate moments included socially awkward Bush making no attempt to hide his apparent boredom by looking at his watch; with the candidates seated on stools, Bush stood up as a question was asked and very obviously stretched out his right arm to check the time.

Clinton beat Bush 370-168. Perot got no electoral votes but received almost 20 million votes in an impressive performance.

1996 Election

The Republicans had made sweeping gains in the 1994 congressional elections with their 'Contract with America', and Bill Clinton was in danger of looking irrelevant.

Never write Clinton off. He recovered to win the 1996 election, beating Bob Dole 379-159, and went on to survive impeachment over his sex scandal involving Monica Lewinsky, with the very clever man at one complicated stage saying, 'It depends upon what the meaning of the word "is" is.'

Clinton survived.

In his second inaugural address, Clinton said, 'At this last Presidential inauguration of the 20th century, let us lift our eyes toward the challenges that await us in the next century.'

2000 Election

George W. Bush once called his younger brother Jeb 'the great governor of Texas' in April 2000. Great or not, Jeb was governor of Florida. George W. also knew the governor of Texas at that time: himself.[13]

In his capacity as governor, Dubya oversaw 152 executions, including that of double-murderer Jonathan Wayne Nobles in 1998. Strapped to the gurney in the death chamber for the lethal injection, Nobles joked to a person watching the execution, 'Steve, it took me this to get you in a suit coat.'[14]

As for the election, the 36-day dispute over Florida's votes triggered seemingly endless legal, political and constitutional rows over what votes could or couldn't be recounted as the nation came to learn of 'hanging chads' or 'dimpled chads'. Voting officials resorted to magnifying glasses to examine a hole on a punch-card ballot paper and see how far it had been punched through by voters using old-fashioned electoral machinery. There were also complaints about unclear ballot papers – far more Democrats accidentally voted twice than Republicans – and constant demands for full or partial recounts in all of the state or specific counties. The national result came down to who had won this mess.

The Florida fiasco ended with the conservative-dominated Supreme Court deciding it did, after all, like interfering in state matters and overruling the Florida Supreme Court, which had ordered a recount of sorts. With almost six million votes cast, Bush and Gore ended with 48.8 per cent each, and Bush officially won the Florida election by only 537 votes or 2,912,790 to 2,912,253 – 48.85 per cent to 48.84 per cent. That gave him the state's 25 votes to win the Electoral College 271-266. Later research said

Bush had won the state anyway based on the votes cast – although, this being Florida, there were some big caveats. The Republican campaign itself had been rocked right at the end with Bush's drink driving arrest from 1976, when he was 30, coming to light. Bush had long given up alcohol when he became president.

In his inaugural address, Bush thanked 'Vice President Gore for a contest conducted with spirit and ended with grace'.

2004 Election

In the first election since the 9/11 attacks, George W. Bush beat John Kerry 286-251 in a close race, though he won by around three million votes.

In his inaugural address, Bush said, 'My most solemn duty is to protect this nation and its people from further attacks and emerging threats. Some have unwisely chosen to test America's resolve, and have found it firm. We will persistently clarify the choice before every ruler and every nation: the moral choice between oppression, which is always wrong, and freedom, which is eternally right.'

2008 Election

Biden's bid for the 2008 nomination wasn't helped by his awkward description of Obama as the 'first sort of mainstream African American who is articulate and bright and clean and a nice-looking guy'. He later apologised.

McCain later regretted choosing Palin as his running mate, even if the Alaska governor didn't literally utter the much ridiculed remark 'I can see Russia from my house'.

Palin actually said there was a remote part of Alaska from where you could see Russia, but, as a campaign rule, if you need to get the atlas out to prove your point you're losing votes.

The 71-year-old McCain was one of the most open candidates in living memory. In response to a question in a high school as to whether he was worried about his memory at his age, McCain said that 'his children have joked about their father "hiding his own Easter eggs,"' and finished his answer with, 'Thanks for the question, you little jerk … You're drafted.'[15]

Obama won 365-173. His '53 per cent of the popular vote was the highest for any Democrat since Lyndon Johnson, and he was the first since Jimmy Carter' to top 50 per cent. 'For almost 60 years, the only Democrats who could win the White House were white southerners. In the end, Obama won by nearly 10 million votes.'[16]

In his inaugural address, Obama said, 'On this day, we gather because we have chosen hope over fear, unity of purpose over conflict and discord.'

2012 Election

Obama faced Utah Senator Mitt Romney in the 2012 election. Extremely competent, an impressive organiser, good looking and from a loving family background, Romney appeared to have it all.

His biggest gaffe to emerge in the campaign was a recording found by American magazine *Mother Jones* in which Romney said, 'There are 47 per cent of the people who will vote for the president no matter what' and that this 47 per cent 'are dependent upon government' and 'believe that they are victims'.

Some attention also focused on Irish setter Seamus, the family dog who was put on the car roof during a long journey for a family holiday way back in 1983 and did not seem to like it. It wasn't literally strapped down but in a carrier on the roof. It inspired Devo's protest song 'Don't Roof Rack Me Bro! (Remember Seamus)'.

Obama beat Romney 332-206 for a second term.

2016 Election

Fewer than 39,000 voters switching from Trump to the Democrats in three key battleground states in 2016 would have made Hillary Clinton president in an election where almost 130 million people voted.[17]

Texas Senator Ted Cruz and Trump were both involved in the race for the Republican nomination. Trump routinely called Cruz 'Lyin' Ted', but nobody expected this (outrageous) headline: 'Trump accuses Cruz's father of helping JFK's assassin'. There appeared to be bad feelings and 'Trump's tangent followed his rebuke of Rafael Cruz using the pulpit to court evangelicals for his son'.[18]

Trump went on to pull off one of the biggest shocks in American political history by winning 304-227.

Clinton, to be fair, suffered a devastating 'October Surprise' which few candidates would have survived – even Bill Clinton would have struggled. The Hillary Clinton camp got the news during a campaign flight when press aide Nick Merrill 'was in the back of the plane with the press when Chris Megerian of the *Los Angeles Times* asked whether he had any response to the reopening of the FBI's investigation into Hillary's handling of sensitive e-mails (as Secretary of State). "Very funny", Merrill replied, thinking it was a joke. Megerian assured him it was not.'[19]

Perhaps with the 2020 campaign in mind, New York born-and-bred Trump switched his primary residence in 2019 from Manhattan's Trump Tower to his Mar-a-Lago resort in Palm Beach, Florida.

New York Governor Andrew Cuomo hid his grief well by tweeting 'Good riddance'.[20]

Election Night:
By the Dawn's Early Light

Joe Biden has pledged to serve only one term if elected, and Donald Trump no more than three.

Constitutional quips aside, there is genuine non-partisan speculation that Biden could declare himself in advance to be a one-term president, as James Polk did in the 1840s, despite the considerable risk of being seen as a lame-duck leader before even taking the oath.[1]

Polk wisely used the resulting freedom of not being worried about re-election to great effect.[2] President Biden would more likely make a one-term-only decision after assessing the first term. But the choice may prove simpler in the coronavirus era, involving as it does brutal economic decisions, according to one political MasterChef: 'The reality is that anyone taking the office of the presidency on Jan. 20, 2021 may well be called upon to do things that would effectively limit them to one term.'[3]

Triple-Teflon-coated Trump has expressed light-hearted interest in being in office for the men's football 2026 World Cup, which will be hosted by the United States, Canada and Mexico, the last two not always Trump's favourite countries. Staying past a Constitution-defying second term, ending in January 2025, has been more than a one-off joke for Trump. Some ultra-Trumpists claim his first term was damaged by what they saw as a politically motivated impeachment attempt.

Donald the Third

Third things first: if Trump wins and has a successful second term – as defined by himself, so we already know it will be – would he be tempted to go for a third term even though he can't?

Tertiary temptations faced presidents like Thomas Jefferson and Theodore Roosevelt (technically it would have been a second full term for Our Teddy) in 1808 and 1908 respectively. Both men chose not to run even though they could – it was simply frowned upon after the two-term example of the great George Washington. Dwight Eisenhower was unable to run again in 1960, when he would have almost certainly won, because of the 22nd Amendment. This prohibits anyone being elected president more than twice and was intended by the Republicans as punishment for FDR's long reign.

Even if he wanted to, it would be close to impossible for Trump to get the 22nd Amendment repealed in time for him to enjoy a third term. The simpler option is to become president for life, and Trump joked about that too when praising Chinese leader Xi Jinping's remarkable job security and remarking, 'Maybe we'll have to give that a shot someday.' Just to be clear, that's also not going to happen.

'He's done WHAT?'

Even if Trump loses on 3 November, he will stay president until Inauguration Day on 20 January. Note to congressional leaders, prime ministers, presidents and the World Health Organisation: keep your phones on over Christmas.

How would Trump react to defeat in 2020? Watch out for major news and dramatic developments on the following days: 4 November, 5 November, 6 November, 7 November … you get the idea.

If Biden loses, the post-mortem begins immediately in the Democratic Party along with the race to find the 2024 candidate. How would the party react to another defeat in 2020? Watch out for major news and dramatic developments on the following days: 4 November, 5 November, 6 November, 7 November … you still get the idea.

The difference, of course, is that if Trump decides to do something in his final 11 weeks in power, then he will simply do it. There is none of the brutality of the British system, in which the dreaded removal van soon arrives outside 10 Downing Street to take away the outgoing prime minister's favourite toys.

If Trump loses, there'll be a lot of quality sulking time for the president as he mulls over declaring his birthday a national holiday, petitioning the Supreme Court for a recount and lobbying to replace Thomas Jefferson at the one place where workers once legally sat on a president's face – Mount Rushmore – 'for a lunch of meatloaf sandwiches if lucky'.[4] Trump hasn't proposed any of these so far, but give him time.

More seriously, it's a safe bet that Trump would neither be a quiet 'outgoing president' before Inauguration Day nor a peaceful 'former president' after 20 January. Just as Barack Obama has criticised aspects of Trump's policy despite the usual silent protocol of former presidents, Trump would find it hard to resist attacking both his successor Biden and predecessor Obama, as well as Obama's predecessor George W. Bush, and Bush's predecessor Bill Clinton, reserving praise only for Obama's successor and Biden's predecessor.

Return to Sender

So will it be a new Democratic dawn as a winner emerges on Wednesday 4 November, or continued Republican presidential rule? Before the sun rises to reveal America's choice, let's go back to some unknowns in the run-up to the election and identify what to look out for on Election Night itself.

More than any president in living memory, Trump has gained political advantage from not being judged on the facts. The endless personal insults aimed at Trump – though he is not exactly innocent himself on this front – often mention his unorthodox hair and purported orange hue. One result of the abuse is that he has regularly escaped having to answer fact-based zingers, and when they do come he plays to his passionate band of followers by blaming 'fake news' and other conspiracies. Some other players in the 2020 campaign were not so lucky, such as the Leap Day dart *The Economist* threw at former Democratic contender Bernie Sanders: 'During 30 years in Congress he has been primary sponsor of just seven bills that became law, two of which concerned the renaming of post offices in Vermont.'[5]

Trump has been deeply fortunate in avoiding brilliant campaigners like Bill Clinton or Obama. Trailing in the polls against Biden, he could once more be rescued by the people who despise him the most as his base hardens, swing voters are put off by over-the-top attacks and others feel strangely drawn to their enemy's enemy.

The same could also happen for Biden, of course.

Wild Cards

Apart from more tear gas being used on protesters ahead of Trump holding up a Bible outside a church, campaign wild cards in 2020 to look out for include a vaccine for coronavirus being announced anywhere on the planet during the final weeks of campaigning. It would obviously do Trump's political health the world of good.

An extreme wild card has a candidate out of contention before Election Day due to illness, death or (alleged) bad behaviour, but not necessarily in that order. Chapter 4 looked at what would happen in the event of illness or worse. Trump is entirely unpredictable. He is the only president who could announce plans to knock down the White House for luxury apartments (there are no such plans) and be taken seriously.

One potential 'October Surprise': very good or extremely bad third-quarter GDP initial figures, released on the Thursday (29 October) before the final weekend of campaigning. Even if misleading, any rise at all in the country's gross domestic product, an old-fashioned barometer of economic health, will be hailed as a miracle by Trump after 40 million Americans were jobless almost halfway through pandemic-hit 2020. Trump can hope for a 'V', where the economy sharply recovers after a severe decline, and Biden will be aided by signs of an 'L' taking shape with the economy unable to pick up. Believe me, nobody gains from an upside-down 'G'.

Biden His Time

The economy beats everything else for voters even if they say it doesn't. If the economy takes an even worse turn in the run-up to Election Day, Biden can just stay in his Delaware basement and say nothing at all. Indeed, early presidents came to power this way when it was considered undignified to plead for votes.

On Election Day itself, wild cards include the effects on turnout of social distancing, bad weather hitting key states (picture storms on the eastern United States helping to win the popular vote for Trump), length of queues to vote (often linked to the number of polling stations) and any interference in what's been called 'hacking the vote' from within America or abroad. Biden winning Idaho or Trump taking D.C. would be a clear sign of something fishy going on.

Black Lives Matter

The 'Black Lives Matter' movement matters a lot to both candidates amid the fallout of nationwide riots and protests after George Floyd's shocking death. The political impact of demonstrations against decades of police brutality could go either way – widespread voter disgust at racist cops and at Trump fanning the flames with needlessly provocative statements, or Trump gaining from public order concerns among mainstream voters over violence by a minority of protesters and sympathy for the majority of decent, brave police officers. Copying Richard Nixon in troubled 1968, Trump has already called himself the 'law and order' president.

Swing voters will have the final say, and it could just be that Trump is a 'lucky' politician, with events going his way (however dreadfully) at the opportune time to gain a small but decisive political advantage in key states. Note what actually happened in 1968 when 'the most determining subject on the minds of voters was race', not the Vietnam War, in the year Revd Martin Luther King Jr was murdered. Sadly it's not what you think: 'The gains of blacks during the period 1960–1968 had aroused powerful resentments among the white population.'[6]

Lots of Money

Coronavirus looks like hanging around long enough to prevent a normal election with party conventions and rallies. Much of the focus will be on an expensive TV campaign. That favours Trump as an incumbent able to raise big bucks and dominate the news agenda.

Both party conventions were planned for August 2020 but with a vastly reduced attendance. Put back from July, a smattering of Democrats meet in Milwaukee in swing state Wisconsin (10 votes) before a few Republicans gather in Charlotte, North Carolina (15 votes), another state up for grabs.

In 2016, the Republicans were the first to meet, in Cleveland, Ohio (18 electoral votes), and the Democrats held their convention in Philadelphia, Pennsylvania (20). Both states were won by Trump. If Hillary Clinton had won the pair, she would have prevailed 270-268 overall.[7]

One question being asked around the world: Will the election definitely take place on 3 November? Yes.

Americans are a can-do and naturally optimistic people, shown nicely by historian Richard Hofstadter's description of a famous Founding Father: 'Through all Jefferson's work there runs like a fresh underground stream the deep conviction that all will turn out well, that life will somehow assert itself.'[8]

They're also a tough bunch. The United States voted in 1864 during a Civil War with a far higher death toll than coronavirus (for now at least).[9]

For 2020, both parties appear to agree that lots of mail-in ballots – using the post to avoid turning up in person on Election Day – look like helping Biden, though it's not clear why, and the quality of debate regarding this issue can quickly deteriorate. Democrats will say Republicans fear democracy. Republicans will say Democrats cheat. Democrats will say Republicans eat little children. Republicans will say Democrats don't go to the dentist. Well, maybe not exactly, but politics at this level has always been unpleasant with the stakes so high.

Bad Boys

Behaviour outside Washington has often been just as bad, however, and elections are a good opportunity to keep everything in perspective. In 1941, Texas governor and prolific biscuit-passer W. Lee 'Pappy' O'Daniel deliberately nominated an extremely frail 86-year-old Andrew Jackson Houston, son of the actual Sam Houston, to fill an interim vacancy in the U.S. Senate. O'Daniel hoped to occupy the seat himself later on. Houston 'at the time of his swearing in, was the oldest man, at eighty-seven, ever to enter the Senate'.[10] The valiant Houston 'answered the call to duty, travelled to the nation's capital, took the oath of office, attended one committee meeting, and passed away a short time later'.[11]

There are Trumpian overtones in O'Daniel, a fascinating and flawed character who used the media – in his case radio – to build a political career. The former flour salesman extraordinaire then beat no less a figure than Lyndon B. Johnson in a special election but was an embarrassing failure when he got to the U.S. Senate. That's where the comparisons end. Love him or loathe him, Trump is one of only five people alive to have served as president of the United States.[12]

Election Night

O'Daniel miraculously found the extra votes he needed to beat LBJ. There'll be none of that old-fashioned wholesome skulduggery in 2020, but with 50 state contests it's hard to predict a time for declaring a winner. Note too that mail-in ballots, if the race is very close, could potentially extend the outcome for a day or more.

With first results coming in after midnight UK time, either retire to bed early on 3 November and rise well before dawn, or go the distance as America makes its crucial decision. Take this BBC advice from the last election: 'As for the final result? Stay glued to your phone or TV or set your alarm for 23:00 EST (04:00 GMT). That's when West Coast polls close and history suggests a winner's declared. It was bang on the hour in 2008, and 15 minutes later in 2012.'[13]

2016 turned out to be after 7 a.m. U.K. time, with Clinton conceding around the bottom of the hour, but in a closer election. See Dave Leip's superb uselectionatalas. org for a timeline of the last election.[14]

Keep an eye out for turnout, typically around the 55 to 60 per cent mark for presidential elections. As a general rule, the higher the turnout, the better the result for the angry candidate. This time round Trump may lose out in comparison to 2016 when he was the trailblazer for the ignored blue-collar workers of America – or grand exploiter, depending on your politics.

Turnout will also have a significant influence on other elections being held the same day, such as all seats in the House of Representatives, currently controlled by the Democrats (hence Trump's impeachment) and around a third of the Senate, currently controlled by the Republicans (hence Trump's acquittal). Those results, almost more than anything else, will help to determine the next president's success or failure in enacting major change.

Watch out for too early signs of overconfidence, including in 2016 when the Hillary Clinton camp reportedly thought Florida was 'in the bank'. According to CBS, 'The Clinton campaign says that they believe they have banked such a big early vote with new Hispanic voters who have never voted before that even if Donald Trump had huge numbers at the polls there's no way he could win that state.'[15] Trump won Florida, and it will be very close this time around. Hey, it's Florida!

Xs in Texas

While a tie would be fun, and a first since the 1800 election, what about clear indications of one candidate doing well?

The whispers are getting louder. If Biden wins Republican stronghold Texas – he surely won't, but it's moving much closer than Trump would ever want – we know the overall winner. If Texas says it is Joe, it ain't gonna be Donald.

Minnesota was surprisingly close last time for such a Democratic fortress. Biden should win there and comfortably. If he doesn't, or only wins narrowly, it will be a bad night for the Democrats.

If Biden regains North Carolina for the Democrats, Trump will be troubled. Trump should win Arizona, even though the state is changing. Ohio is always one to watch as the state has an impressive record of choosing the overall winner.

If Trump were to win Pennsylvania again, that's pretty bad for Biden, who was born in the state. Michigan, the site of a coronavirus standoff, also offers a good hint to the eventual result. Trump won there last time but voters may think he has not come through with the promised revival, for a variety of reasons, and respond accordingly.

Trump could win overall by 40 to 50 electoral votes but not many more. If voters have finally had enough of the Offender-in-Chief, with too many different communities, groups, races, genders and interest groups insulted too many times, Biden could wallop Trump and win by north of 150.

But Trump is a better campaigner than Biden, and always remember that the sitting president usually wins.

O Come All Ye Faithless

Move on to 14 December, when each state's electors meet. If the result is very close in electoral votes, and the 'loser' has again won the popular vote, some electors could proudly add the tag 'faithless' to their names by not voting for the candidate they're meant to support in the modern understanding of their role.

It would be a huge shock if faithless electors changed the actual outcome. The question will be whether in practice the 2020 Supreme Court ruling prohibits the act itself, allows state punishment after the act or both. A fine is not going to change the result, though forcing states to replace faithless electors could. What if a Democratic-controlled state didn't want to punish a faithless elector for not supporting a Republican, or the other way round?

That's assuming the replacements behaved themselves – and who would replace the replacements if they didn't? And so it goes on. It's worth noting that crowdfunding to pay the fines of faithless electors who put Trump out of office would easily reach hundreds of millions of dollars. That wouldn't necessarily make it right.

It's an increasingly toxic political atmosphere, with unexpected twists set to be as startling in America as 'Man accidentally ejects himself from fighter jet during surprise flight' was in France.[16] While an all-out electoral rebellion would only have a chance to happen if the race was very close, this much is clear: if it was going to happen in any presidential election, it would be this one. The poor man, by the way, 'had never expressed any desire to fly in a fighter jet'.

Should populist Trump not be so popular and lose in 2020, don't be too surprised to hear 'I'll be back'. A sprightly 78 years old by 2024, Trump would be unlikely to win Republican backing again, though not all agree. It is universally agreed, however, that not even Trump would have the cheek to seek the Democratic nomination. An 'Again Make America Great Again' (AMAGA) third party challenge from Trump – similar to the rebellious spirit of Teddy Roosevelt's Bull Moose run in 1912 – is a possibility.[17] It would almost certainly be unsuccessful, and offer a huge incentive to Biden to run in '24 as an incumbent president, because the opposition vote would be split.

2024 and Beyond

Prediction time: the 2020s will see the first all-female presidential race, and the early 2030s possibly all four women on the two tickets.

The media has noticed that one politician, New York Representative Alexandria Ocasio-Cortez, has already joined the Democratic pantheon of politicians best known by their initials, alongside FDR (Franklin Delano Roosevelt), JFK (John F. Kennedy) and LBJ (Lyndon Baines Johnson). It's a big leap of faith to go from 'All the way with LBJ' to 'AOK with AOC', but it might be narrowing each year. The author declares he has no financial interest in 'AOC Is AOK!' merchandise already available.

Like Ocasio-Cortez, Bill Clinton was once seen as the up-and-coming star in the Democratic Party. A governor of a small southern state, Arkansas, Clinton was more 'moderate' by American standards than AOC as he became the third-youngest president at 46. Four years from now, Ocasio-Cortez will just be old enough to go for the Democratic presidential nomination after becoming the youngest-ever woman elected to the U.S. Congress at age 29 in 2018.

That may seem far-fetched – and a race for the U.S. Senate a more likely outcome for AOC – but winning the presidency wouldn't be her biggest political upset.[18] In the Democratic primary to choose the party's candidate for a safe congressional seat, Ocasio-Cortez defeated Joe Crowley, a powerful high-ranking Democrat. A neutral observer of American politics, one Mr Trump of Washington, rejoiced in the defeat of 'Big Trump Hater Congressman Joe Crowley' and said, 'Perhaps he should have been nicer, and more respectful, to his President!'

A democratic socialist with a great bilingual back story as a community activist and Manhattan bartender, AOC may still be too left wing for mainstream America voters – the 'S' word is the big problem for most states – but there's time for either AOC or America to adapt.

The Constitution requires the president to be at least 35 on taking office. There's nothing in the Constitution preventing any writer from padding out his last chapter in a desperate race against time by quoting the Constitution, so here for possibly the fifth and final time is the relevant age section: Article II, Section 1 of the Constitution says nobody can be eligible for president without having 'attained to the Age of thirty five Years, and been fourteen Years a Resident within the United States'.

Exit Men

In the event of Biden losing to Trump in 2020, the '24 presidential candidate picked by the Democrats will likely be a woman and from a much younger generation with a distinct political vocabulary. If AOC seeks and wins the Democratic nomination in 2024, the 2020 election may gain enormous retrospective significance as the very last race without a woman running for the top job.

If she won in 2024 – and it would arguably be less of a surprise than Trump's revolutionary win in 2016 – AOC would become the first female president, the youngest president and, lest we forget all the blood, toil, sweat and tears involved in Chapter 3, the president with the longest surname.

It may turn out to be even more significant than that by ushering in domination by female politicians. Come 2021, the last 59 elections will have been won by a man.

The same success for women would mean men having to wait until 2260 to make a comeback by courting votes in the top three Electoral College states: Texas, a warmed-up Alaska and Mars.

The Electoral College

What's the immediate future for the Electoral College?

Another disputed election result in 2020, where Trump again wins with fewer votes than his opponent and gloats excessively about it, could trigger an increase in the number of states committing to the National Popular Vote project.

More likely in a conservative country which reveres its past – Confederate statues no longer counting – America will keep its Electoral College. Numbers wise, Texas is tipped to pick up three more votes for the 2024 and '28 elections, moving into the prestigious 40s with 41 votes, and heading for swing-state status. That's where it starts to get intriguing. If Texas opts to back the NPV bill, the revolution will be close.

Florida is set to gain two votes, increasing from 29 to 31. California and New York could drop by one, to 54 and 28, respectively, based on initial results from the U.S. 2020 Census, which determines the number of representatives in a state and hence the Electoral College slice. Texas will remain the second-biggest state and Florida will become the third-largest state in the Electoral College, with New York down to fourth.[19]

Bedtime Story

If Trump wins, he will have no need to worry about securing a further term or pleasing voters. It's possible that America and the world have so far only seen his shy, kind, gentle side. Get ready for an unrestrained President Donald J. Trump ready to speak his mind.

Thank you for reading along. It's getting late, so let's end with a bedtime story.

No tale better illustrates the occasionally wild world of American politics and history than the purported reaction of one man back in the 19th century to the famous Monroe Doctrine. About to be murdered by an impassioned mob (it's an adult bedtime story), the man pleads for his life: 'I didn't say I was against the Monroe Doctrine; I love the Monroe Doctrine, I would die for the Monroe Doctrine. I merely said I didn't know what it was.'[20]

Hopefully many more readers now know what the Electoral College is. I wouldn't worry too much about any mob – let's be honest, it's still quite a boring subject.

Notes

Introduction: Tuesday, Tuesday

1. Washington, D.C. (District of Columbia) has been included in the Electoral College since the 1964 election after the 23rd Amendment was ratified in 1961.
2. The Electoral College has been 538 votes since 1964. If you did want to play the game, add the top six states' total of 191 to the next highest five of Ohio (18), Georgia (16), Michigan (16), North Carolina (15) and New Jersey (14). You have reached 270 from only 11 states.
3. 'Although the term is not found in the Constitution, the electors have been known collectively as the Electoral College since the early days of the republic, an expression that may be misleading, since the college has no continuing existence…and ceases to exist immediately after the electors have performed their function,' Thomas H. Neale, *CRS Report for Congress: The Electoral College: How It Works in Contemporary Presidential Elections, 2012,* Congressional Research Service, footnote, p 1.
4. Full list of states and their electoral votes for the 2020 election at http://archives.gov/electoral-college/allocation.
5. The 'First Tuesday after First Monday' rule means Election Day always falls anywhere from 2 to 8 November.
6. All calculations depend on how much travel was involved, of course, but it appears less clear whether Friday was ever

considered as a serious possibility. Some campaigners now want elections moved to the weekend to make it easier to vote and increase turnout. A proposed Weekend Voting Act backed 'the first Saturday and Sunday after the first Friday in November'.

7. Robert M. Alexander, *Representation and the Electoral College* (New York: Oxford University Press, 2019), p. 14.

8. Paul Finkelman, 'The Proslavery Origins of the Electoral College', *Cardoza Law Review*, 2002, Vol. 23:4, pp. 1, 145; Joseph E. Kallenbach, 'Recent Proposals to Reform the Electoral College System', *The American Political Science Review*, Vol. 30, No. 5, October 1936, p. 928.

9. From about 122 million in 1929 to around 330 million in 2020.

10. Jacob Weisberg, *George W. Bushisms* (New York: Fireside, 2001), p. 18. Iraq aside, if that's ever possible, Bush had a nice dry sense of humour as president but in this quote he was just expressing his pro-fish sentiments.

11. The numbers don't add up to 538 as seven so-called 'faithless electors' voted for a different candidate. More on this species in Chapter 4, *O Ye of Little Fish: Problems with the Electoral College*.

12. 'How Trump could lose by 5 million votes and still win in 2020', nbcnews.com, 19/7/2019.

13. This doesn't count JFK's complicated win over Nixon (see 1960 election in Chapter 7).

14. William Cummings, 'Trump says he's "so great looking and smart, a true Stable Genius" in tweet bashing 2020 Dems', *USA Today*, 11/7/2019.

15. Donald Trump Jr.'s tweet was on 9/2/2020.

16. archives.gov/electoral-college/electors.

17. See more sensitive coverage of his death in Chapter 5.

18. In a nice twist, William H. Rehnquist, the presiding Chief Justice in the Bush-backing Supreme Court case, wrote a book on the 1876 controversy, *Centennial Crisis: The Disputed Election of 1876* (New York: Vintage Books, 2005).

19. Now impossible under the 22nd Amendment.

20. Lyndon Johnson holds the record percentage of the popular vote at 61.1 per cent in his 486-52 win over Barry Goldwater.

1 Donald Duck: Why Trump Ignores California

1. In the past Trump has blamed energy-efficient light bulbs for his distinctive skin hue, perhaps jokingly, while adding they're not very good anyway.
2. Article II, Section 1 of the United States Constitution. Vice presidents must also be at least 35 as they have to be eligible to be president. Biden, whose birthday is 20 November, will be 78 by Inauguration Day in January.
3. The author was also extremely late in finishing the manuscript as he found the subject very hard to understand.
4. 'Why HuffPost's Presidential Forecast Didn't See A Donald Trump Win Coming', huffingtonpost.co.uk, 10/11/2016, updated 3/1/2017. Mixing real regret with parenthetical protest, the *HuffPost* conceded its 98 per cent figure 'was more pro-Clinton than most other forecast models (although all of them predicted a Clinton win)'.
5. Robert M. Alexander, *Representation and the Electoral College* (New York: Oxford University Press, 2019), p. 3.
6. From *The Stevenson Wit: Selections from famous Speeches, Press Conferences and Off-the-Cuff Remarks*, LP record narrated by David Brinkley, RCA Victor Red Seal, 1965.
7. Stephen Ambrose, *Nixon: The Education of a Politician 1913-62* (London: Simon and Schuster, 1987), p. 671.
8. Sami Sparber, 'New polls point to Texas as swing state in 2020', *Houston Chronicle*, 19/6/2019.
9. Kristian Ramos, 'Latino Support for Trump Is Real: And that's a problem for Democrats', *The Atlantic*, 17/2/2020.
10. Sam Roberts, 'Infamous 'Drop Dead' Was Never Said by Ford', *The New York Times*, 28/12/2006. The *Daily News* edition was 30/10/1975.
11. Andrew Meyer, 'The South (or the North, or the West…) Will Rise Again, and Again, and Again: Viewing the Electoral College from the Perspective of Chinese History', Chapter 4, p. 13, in Eric Burin (ed.), *Picking the President: Understanding the Electoral College* (Grand Forks: The Digital Press, 2017).
12. Matt Pearce, 'How Faith Spotted Eagle became the first

Native American to win an electoral vote for president', *Los Angeles Times*, 20/12/2016.

13. A state's longest serving senator gets the senior tag, in Vermont's case 80-year-old Patrick Leahy.

14. Rob Brunner, 'Ralph Nader Is Opening Up About His Regrets', washingtonian.com/2019/11/03/ralph-nader-is-opening-up-about-his-regrets/, 3/11/2019. It makes painful reading for Nader fans.

15. Elizabeth Wasserman, 'Trump Says Pence Is on 2020 Ticket: 'He's Our Man, 100 per cent', bloomberg.com, 22/11/2019.

16. Biden, as Obama's vice president, did not seek the 2016 nomination which he understandably attributed to the death of his son Beau in 2015 at the age of 46. He would have faced a formidable challenge from frontrunners Hillary Clinton and Bernie Sanders. Evan Osnos, 'Why Biden Didn't Run', www.newyorker.com/news/news-desk/why-biden-didnt-run, 21/10/2015.

17. All quotes from Martin Plissner, *The Control Room: How Television Calls the Shots in Presidential Elections* (New York: Touchstone, 2000), p. 132.

18. From the Commission on Presidential Debates: debates.org/voter-education/debate-transcripts/october-6-1976-debate-transcript/

19. During his doomed campaign for the 1988 Democratic nomination, Biden was found to have used lines by Britain's Labour leader Neil Kinnock in a speech, including 'first Kinnock/Biden in a thousand generations' to go to university/college. 'The Reagan Question' is regularly used in election campaigns when presidents are struggling.

20. https://edition.cnn.com/videos/politics/2011/06/09/vault.debate.no.jack.kennedy.ktvk. Contains distressing scenes: Not to be watched with children present.

2 How It All Began: The Birth of the Electoral College

1. Nancy Finlay, 'Nathan Hale: The Man and the Legend', connecticuthistory.org/nathan-hale-the-man-and-the-legend/.

Born in Coventry, Connecticut, Hale was designated the official state hero in 1985.

2. theconstitutional.com/blog/2016/03/15/independence-hall-history.

3. David O. Stewart, *The Summer of 1787* (New York: Simon & Schuster, 2007), p. 155.

4. C. S. Potts, 'Abolition of the Electoral College', *The Southwestern Political and Social Science Quarterly*, Vol. 7, No. 3, December 1926, p. 253.

5. Both quotes from William P. Kladky, mountvernon. org/library/digitalhistory/digital-encyclopedia/article/ constitutional-convention/.

6. Neil L. York, 'The First Continental Congress and the Problem of American Rights', *The Pennsylvania Magazine of History and Biography*, Vol. 122, No. 4, October 1998, p. 355.

7. Theodore Draper, *A Struggle for Power: The American Revolution* (London: Little, Brown, 1996), p. 502.

8. Robert Middlekauff, *The Glorious Cause: The American Revolution, 1763-89* (New York: Oxford University Press, 1985), p. 317.

9. Edmund S. Morgan, *The Birth of the Republic: 1763-89* (Chicago: The University of Chicago Press, 1992), p. 107.

10. Gordon S. Wood, *The American Revolution: A History* (New York: Modern Library, 2003), p. 151.

11. Todd Estes, 'The Connecticut Effect: The Great Compromise of 1787 and the History of Small State Impact on Electoral College Outcomes', *The Historian*, Vol. 73, No. 2, Summer 2011, p. 256.

12. George C. Edwards III, *Why the Electoral College Is Bad for America* (New Haven: Yale University Press, 2004), pp. 90-91.

13. Louis Fisher, *The Constitution Between Friends: Congress, the President and the Law* (New York: St. Martin's Press, 1978), p. 9.

14. Stewart, *The Summer of 1787*, p. 29. In *To America: Personal Reflections of An Historian* (New York: Simon & Schuster, 2003), p. 11, Stephen Ambrose notes 'Of the nine Presidents who owned slaves, only Washington freed

his'. His footnote names the nine as Washington, Thomas Jefferson, James Madison, James Monroe, Andrew Jackson, William Henry Harrison, John Tyler, James Polk and Franklin Pierce.

15. Pauline Maier (introduction) in *The Declaration of Independence and The Constitution of the United States* (New York: Bantam Books, 1998), p. 30.

16. Maier, *The Declaration of Independence and The Constitution,* p. 30.

17. Number LXVIII, *The Federalist Papers: James Madison, Alexander Hamilton and John Jay*, edited by Isaac Kramnick (London: Penguin Books, 1987), p. 395.

18. Ben Macintyre, 'Public life, private moments' in 'Obama: Behind the scenes at the Inauguration' supplement, *The Times*, 24/1/2009, p. 2.

19. Alistair Cooke, *Alistair Cooke's America* (London: Book Club Associates, 1981), p. 145. It's arguable that no British-born writer has known America in more depth than Cooke and it was a grisly end to a distinguished career: 'Alistair Cooke's body snatcher apologises', telegraph.co.uk/news/2119443/Alistair-Cookes-body-snatcher-apologises.html, 13/6/2008.

20. Charles O. Jones, *The American Presidency: A Very Short Introduction* (New York: Oxford University Press, 2007), p. 43.

3 Mr Tall Goes to Washington

1. Ford remains the only president never to have been elected even as vice president (see 1976 election in Chapter 7). He changed his name at age 22 to that of a kinder stepfather called Gerald Ford while tweaking the reindeer-themed middle name. Bill Clinton's father, William Jefferson Blythe, died in a car crash three months before the future president was born. Clinton changed his surname from Blythe to Clinton in high school but his stepfather Roger Clinton was not as nice as Ford's.

2. David Boaz, 'RIP Tonie Nathan, the First Woman to Receive an Electoral Vote', cato.org/blog/rip-tonie-nathan-first-woman-receive-electoral-vote, 21/3/2014. Roger MacBride, a man who took his history seriously and also played a key role in bringing *Little House on the Prairie* to TV screens, was the faithless elector.

3. T. A. Frail, 'The Only Time a Major Party Embraced a Third-Party Candidate for President,' smithsonianmag. com, 26/7/2016.

4. A list of presidents and their native states can be found in *Presidential Elections 1789-2008* (Washington, D.C.: CQ Press, 2010), p. 3.

5. As governor, Wilson signed into law California's notorious '3 strikes and you're out' penal policy in 1994 which attracted global headlines the following year when 'Jerry Dewayne Williams was sentenced to prison for 25 years to life for stealing a slice of pepperoni pizza', Eric Slater, *Los Angeles Times*, 3/3/1995. Matt Taibbi looks at the wider issue in 'Cruel and Unusual Punishment: The Shame of Three Strikes Laws', *Rolling Stone*, 27/3/2013, with Taibbi also noting that Williams was released after five years.

6. William A. DeGregorio, *The Complete Book of U.S. Presidents* (New York: Barricade Books, 1996), p. 527. It's a real labour of love and the perfect holiday book if you can fit it in your hand baggage.

7. President William McKinley was shot on 6 September 1901 and died eight days later.

8. S. Jay Olshansky, Hiram Beltran-Sanchez, Bruce A. Carnes, Yang Claire Yang, Yi Li, Bradley Willcox, 'Longevity and Health of U.S. Presidential Candidates for the 2020 Election,' American Federation for Aging Research, afar.org.

9. Aziz Inan, 'Mathematical oddities in memory of President John F. Kennedy', *The Beacon*, 22/11/2017. For really patient readers, there's a twist when JFK turns 199 in 2116: upbeacon.com/article/2017/11/jfk-brainteasers.

10. Some height data in this section comes from potus.com/presidential-facts/presidential-heights/.

11. David Sim, 'In Pictures: Tallest U.S. Presidents in History', *Newsweek*, 23/3/2018.

12. Jay Mathews, 'Is Hillary Clinton getting taller? Or is the Internet getting dumber?' *The Washington Post*, 24/9/2015.

13. Ian Crouch, 'The rise of the anti-Trump "Girthers"', *The New Yorker*, 18/1/2018. Readers wanting more nourishment can consult Erik Kain's article, 'A History of Fat Presidents', Forbes.com, 28/9/2011, which does what it says on the tin.

14. Bruce Handy, 'An Illustrated History of Donald Trump's Hair. Warning! Don't Read Before Lunch!', *Vanity Fair*, 8/9/2015.

15. 'The Official Power Ranking of American Presidential Facial Hair', gq.com/gallery/american-presidents-with-facial-hair, 13/2/2016.

16. Mark Tosh, 'Taking a Closer Look at GOTPOTUS (Glasses of the Presidents of the United States)', visionmonday.com (search GOTPOTUS), 16/2/2018.

17. Information from the table in Eric Ostermeier's 'Presidents Day Special: The Astrological Signs of the presidents', editions.lib.umn.edu/smartpolitics/2010/02/15/presidents-day-special-the-ast/, 15/2/2010.

18. Aine Cain and Samantha Lee, 'A look at the zodiac signs of all the US presidents', businessinsider.com, 1/7/2018.

19. All gold medal figures from olympic.org/united-states-of-america. All 100-metre times, some of which are record-equalling runs, from 'World Record Progression of 100 Metres', worldathletics.org.

20. Webb Garrison, *A Treasury of White House Tales* (Nashville: Rutledge Hill Press, 1996), p. 244.

4 O Ye of Little Fish: Problems with the Electoral College

1. A former speechwriter for Jimmy Carter said the president 'during his first six months in office would personally review all requests to use the White House tennis court'. James Fallows, 'The Passionless Presidency: The trouble with

Jimmy Carter's Administration', *The Atlantic*, May 1979. Carter denied the claim but backtracked slightly later and it was symbolic of a president seemingly over-immersed in detail whilst not seeing the bigger picture. Like most people, Fallows found Carter to be a decent and likeable man.

2. 'Carters recall 1976 Campaign on Presidents Day', Beth Alston/Lisa Law, americustimesrecorder.com/2016/02/18/carters-recall-1976-campaign-on-presidents-day/.

3. Or just a convenient excuse to refry the fish story. Readers and voters must decide for themselves. Herbert Hoover (1929-33) is the fishing-friendliest president so far including a 1963 book *Fishing for fun: And to wash your soul* (available via the Hoover Presidential Library). A famous Hoover quote declares that 'All men are equal before fish'.

4. William G. Mayer, Emmett H. Buell Jr., James E. Campbell, Mark Joslyn, 'The Electoral College and Campaign Strategy', p. 103, in *Choosing a President: The Electoral College and Beyond*, edited by Paul D. Schumaker and Burdett A. Loomis (New York: Seven Bridges Press, 2002).

5. Robert M. Alexander, *Representation and the Electoral College* (New York: Oxford University Press, 2019), p. 9. Against the argument that 'the Electoral College ensures that less populated states cannot be ignored in presidential campaigns', Alexander notes that 'candidates rarely visit sparsely populated states', such as Wyoming and Alaska. That's also on Page 9 but I have read all the book, honest.

6. Jon Meacham, *American Lion: Andrew Jackson in the White House* (New York: Random House, 2009), pp. 25-26.

7. Jackson added to his collection with a slug (removed in 1831) below the left shoulder from 'a gunfight on September 4, 1813 with Thomas Hart Benton and his brother Jesse'. Robert V. Remini, *Andrew Jackson: The Course of American Freedom, 1822-1832*, Volume Two (Baltimore: Johns Hopkins, 1998), p. 2. Thomas Hart Benson's daughter Jessie later eloped to her father's initial fury with John C. Fremont, the famed explorer and very first Republican Party candidate in 1856. If you're going to head off into the great unknown with anyone, 'The Pathfinder' is not a bad choice. 'In spite of all

predictions, the marriage proved very happy', Allan Nevins, *Fremont: Pathmarker of the West* (Lincoln: University of Nebraska Press, 1992), p. 66.

8. Kenneth C. Davis, *Don't Know Much about History* (New York: Avon Books, 1995), p. 423.

9. See Ron Elving, 'The Florida Recount Of 2000: A Nightmare That Goes on Haunting', npr.org, 12/11/2018.

10. Chapter 6, *After the People Vote: A Guide to the Electoral College*, edited by John C. Fortier (Washington D.C.: AEI Press, 2004). Walter Berns edited the first two editions.

11. For the record, they weren't the 29th president's breasts. Harding (1921-23) was writing a love letter on Christmas Eve 1910 to his mistress Carrie Phillips. See Christopher Klein, 'Warren G. Harding's Steamy Love Letters Unsealed', history.com, 29/7/2014, updated 3/8/2018.

12. The helpful stages are outlined by *After the People Vote*, pp. 23-25, with specific dates from Derek T. Muller, Pepperdine University School of Law, in his blog 'Key (sometimes underappreciated) 2020 election dates', excessofdemocracy. com, 13/2/2020.

13. Joshua Tucker, washingtonpost.com/politics/2020/05/16/ what-happens-if-us-presidential-candidate-withdraws-or-dies-before-election-is-over-part-1/, 16/5/2020.

14. *After the People Vote*, p. 25.

15. Brooks Jackson, 'Republicans could block Carnahan's widow if she wins Senate seat', CNN.com, 31/10/2000.

16. Ariane de Vogue, 'Supreme Court appears poised to let states keep "faithless electors" out of the Electoral College', edition.cnn.com/2020/05/13/politics/electoral-college-faithless-electors-supreme-court/index.html.

17. Robert W. Bennett, *Taming the Electoral College* (Stanford: Stanford University Press, 2006), p. 45.

18. Alexander, *Representation and the Electoral College*, p. 183. See, I did read it all. Richard M. Johnson, subject of a race hate campaign, was the vice president involved in 1836.

19. Thomas H. Neale, 'The Electoral College: How It Works in Contemporary Presidential Elections', Congressional Research Service, www.crs.gov, 15/5/2019.

20. Conrad Joyner and Ronald Pedderson, 'The Electoral College Revisited', *The Southwestern Social Science Quarterly*, Vol. 45, No. 1, June 1964, pp. 34-35.

5 Father of the Nation to Uncle Abe: 1789–1864

1. Mary Ann Harrell, 'The Changing White House,' in *The White House: An Historic Guide* (Washington, D.C.: White House Historical Association, 1973), p. 105 (caption).
2. David Reynolds, *America, Empire of Liberty*, Penguin (London: Penguin Books, 2010), p. 85.
3. With apologies to the good folk of South Carolina, whose nickname is of course 'The Palmetto State'. A few states have joined the Union over the decades after a specific election year but still participated in the Electoral College.
4. Sources for presidential results in Chapters 5-7: *Presidential Elections 1789-2008* (Washington, D.C.: CQ Press, 2010); G. Scott Thomas, *The Pursuit of the White House: A Handbook of Presidential Election Statistics and History* (Westport: Greenwood Press, 1987); Larry J. Sabato and Howard R. Ernst, *Encyclopedia of American Political Parties and Elections* (New York: Checkmark Books, 2007); National Archives website archives.gov/electoral-college; Federal Election Commission website fec.gov/introduction-campaign-finance/election-and-voting-information/ (1992-2016); Dave Leip's Atlas of U.S. Presidential Elections, uselectionatlas.org; and 'The American Presidency Project' at UC Santa Barbara, presidency.ucsb.edu/statistics/elections/. For great visuals, see periodicpresidents.com.
5. From inaugural.senate.gov. The verse starts 'Zebulun shall dwell at the haven of the sea', kingjamesbibleonline.org. Theodore Roosevelt didn't use a Bible in 1901 when he was sworn in after McKinley's assassination. John Quincy Adams had a law book.
6. Lionel Elvin, *Men of America* (Harmondsworth: Penguin Books, 1941), p. 62.
7. See www.senate.gov/reference/reference_item/Nine_Capitals_

of_the_United_States.htm from Robert Fortenbaugh's *The Nine Capitals of the United States* (York, Pennsylvania: Maple Press Co, 1948).

8. Jeffrey L. Pasley, *The First Presidential Contest: 1796 and the Founding of American Democracy* (Lawrence: The University Press of Kansas, 2013).

9. George C. Edwards III, *Why the Electoral College Is Bad for America* (New Haven: Yale University Press, 2004), p. 21.

10. Ron Chernow, *Alexander Hamilton* (New York: Penguin Books, 2005), p. 623. Hamilton, who lost his son in a duel, would go on to lose his own life in an 'interview' with Burr in 1804 after upsetting Jefferson's vice president once too often. The Hamilton-Burr duel, including the contention that Hamilton deliberately missed and Burr deliberately aimed, is delightfully detailed by Chernow in Chapter 42, 'Fatal Errand'. Another account of the duel is given in Joseph J. Ellis' Pulitzer Prize-winning *Founding Brothers: The Revolutionary Generation* (London: Faber and Faber, 2002), Chapter 1, 'The Duel'.

11. Bruce Ackerman, *The Failure of the Founding Fathers: Jefferson, Marshall, and the Rise of Presidential Democracy* (Cambridge, Massachusetts: Harvard University Press, 2007), p. 93.

12. John Ferling, *Adams vs. Jefferson: The Tumultuous Election of 1800* (New York: Oxford University Press, 2014), p. 200.

13. All inaugural address excerpts are from the Joint Congressional Committee on Inaugural Ceremonies, inaugural.senate.gov.

14. monticello.org/thomas-jefferson/louisiana-lewis-clark/the-louisiana-purchase/.

15. 'All his life, Madison had been aware of a small stature that required stretching to reach five feet five', A. J. Langguth, *Union 1812: The Americans Who Fought the Second War of Independence* (New York: Simon & Schuster, 2007), p. 197. An unstretched Madison was 5'4" (1.63 meters), though some go as high as 5'6". Johnny Galecki, who plays Dr Leonard Hofstadter, is 5'5".

16. G. Scott Thomas, *The Pursuit of the White House: A Handbook of Presidential Election Statistics and History* (Westport: Greenwood Press, 1987), p. 15.

17. Paul F. Boller Jr., *Presidential Campaigns* (New York: Oxford University Press, 1996) p. 45.

18. Forrest McDonald, *The American Presidency: An Intellectual History* (Lawrence: University Press of Kansas, 1994), p. 430.

19. 'Andrew Jackson holds "open house" at the White House', history.com/this-day-in-history/jackson-holds-open-house-at-the-white-house.

20. James W. Clarke, *American Assassins: The Darker Side of Politics* (Princeton: Princeton University Press, 1982), p. 195. Due to his illness (and because he misfired) Clarke was not held to be criminally responsible.

21. Gail Collins, *William Henry Harrison* (New York: Times Books, 2012), p. 119. Collins points out the president 'was always out in the elements during his early presidency,' including going to a bookshop to buy a Bible for the White House (p. 121).

22. Robert Seager II, *and Tyler too: A Biography of John and Julia Gardiner Tyler* (New York: McGraw-Hill, 1963), p. 103.

23. The tragedy is described in Michael F. Holt, *Franklin Pierce* (New York: Times Books, 2010), p. 50.

24. H. W. Brands, *The Age of Gold* (London: Arrow Books, 2002), p. 364. Any book by Brands is pure gold.

25. Jon Roper, *The Illustrated Encyclopedia of the Presidents of America* (London: Hermes House, 2008), p. 88.

26. Boller, *Presidential Campaigns*, p. 91.

27. Kenneth M. Stampp, *America in 1857: A Nation on the Brink* (New York: Oxford University Press, 1992), p. 113.

28. D. W. Brogan, with preface by Hugh Brogan, *Abraham Lincoln* (London: Gerald Duckworth, 1974), p. 29. First published 1935.

29. David Herbert Donald, *Lincoln* (London: Pimlico, 1995), p. 544.

6 The Drinker to The Thinker: 1868–1944

1. In Grant's case it stood for nothing at all but looked good. Evan Andrews, '10 Things You May Not Know About Ulysses S. Grant', history.com/news/10-things-you-may-not-know-about-ulysses-s-grant, 23/7/2015, updated 7/4/2020. See '25th Amendment' section in Chapter 2 for Truman's problem with the letter 'S'.
2. *Vice Presidents: A Biographical Dictionary*, edited by L. Edward Purcell (New York: Checkmark Books, 2001), p. 149.
3. Robert Dallek, *Hail to the Chief: The Making and Unmaking of American Presidents* (New York: Oxford University Press, 2001), p. 152.
4. Todd Estes, 'The Connecticut Effect: The Great Compromise of 1787 and the History of Small State Impact on Electoral College Outcomes', *The Historian*, Vol. 73, No. 2, Summer 2011, p. 262. For a detailed examination of the 1876 election, see Sidney I. Pomerantz, *Election of 1876*, pp. 168-224, in *The Coming to Power: Critical Presidential Elections in American History*, edited by Arthur M. Schlesinger Jr. (New York: Chelsea House Publishers, 1972).
5. Ted Widmer, 'So Help Me God', *The American Scholar*, Vol. 74, No. 1, Winter 2005, p. 38.
6. Both quotes from Mark Wahlgren Summers, *Rum, Romanism, & Rebellion: The Making of a President 1884* (Chapel Hill: University of North Carolina Press, 2000), pp. 281-82.
7. Daniel Schorr, 'Not Running? Say So, Sherman Style,' NPR News, Weekend Edition, 24/6/2007. He wouldn't have done very well in Georgia, anyway. After easily losing the fight for the 1976 Democratic presidential nomination, Udall is said to have remarked: 'The people have voted (pause). The bastards!' The first person to say this is believed to have been political prankster and operative Dick Tuck after losing a California Senate primary election in 1966.
8. Charles W. Calhoun, *Benjamin Harrison* (New York: Times Books, 2005), p. 58.

9. Paul F. Boller Jr., *Presidential Campaigns* (New York: Oxford University Press, 1996), p. 158.

10. R. Hal Williams, *Realigning America: McKinley, Bryan, and the Remarkable Election of 1896* (Lawrence: University Press of Kansas, 2010), pp. 36-37.

11. L. Sandy Maisel, *American Political Parties and Elections: A Very Short Introduction* (New York: Oxford University Press, 2007), p. 37.

12. James W. Clarke, *American Assassins: The Darker Side of Politics* (Princeton, New Jersey: Princeton University Press, 1982), p. 39. Jump a couple of pages for the anarchist's background at a notoriously tough time for workers in America.

13. William Roscoe Thayer, *Theodore Roosevelt: An Intimate Biography* (New York: Grosset & Dunlap, 1919), p. 243.

14. James Chace, *1912: Wilson, Roosevelt, Taft & Debs – The Election that Changed the Country* (New York: Simon & Schuster, 2005), p. 117.

15. Edward S. Corwin, *Presidential Power and the Constitution*, edited by Richard Loss (Ithaca: Cornell University Press, 1977), p. 42.

16. Martin L. Fausold, *The Presidency of Herbert C. Hoover* (Lawrence: University Press of Kansas, 1988), p. 29.

17. All inaugural address excerpts are from the Joint Congressional Committee on Inaugural Ceremonies, inaugural.senate.gov.

18. Reagan, who likely voted FDR in the 1936 election, said Landon had lived 'half the life of our nation since the framing of the Constitution'. Reagan Library: youtube.com/watch?v=yGq4SghdTTA.

19. Bob Dole, *Great Political Wit: Laughing (Almost) All the Way to the White House* (New York: Broadway Books, 2000), p. 57.

20. William D. Hassett, *Off the Record With F.D.R.: 1942-1945* (London: George Allen & Unwin, 1960), p. 292.

7 When Harry Met Dewey to Enter the Donald: 1948–2016

1. See Nicholas Wapshott, 'Farewell to last Yankee Civil-War Widow', The Times News Service, 20/1/2003.
2. Robert Dallek, *Harry S. Truman* (New York: Times Books, 2008), p. 79.
3. Chester J. Pach Jr., 'Dwight D. Eisenhower: Campaigns and Elections', millercenter.org/president/eisenhower/campaigns-and-elections.
4. The author knows the feeling.
5. *The Kennedy Wit*, edited by Bill Adler (New York: Gramercy, 1964), p. 11.
6. Martin Walker, *The Cold War* (London: Fourth Estate, 1993), p. 189.
7. James Haskins with Kathleen Benson & Ellen Inkelis, *The Great American Crazies* (New York: Condor, 1977), p. 26. Reporting the trial in April 1975, the *New York Times* says the bank note-challenged robber was given $970 and caught shortly after.
8. latimes.com/archives/la-xpm-1987-09-08-vw-6663-story.html
9. Lou Cannon, 'The Truth in Reagan's Humor', *The Washington Post*, 27/4/1987.
10. 'Fall from Grace – Seven days in May end with a front runner's implosion', *Time*, 18/5/1987, p. 6. Both Hart and Rice denied any affair. The 2018 film, *The Front Runner*, starring Hugh Jackman, is about the scandal and media attitudes at the time. See also Alan Dundes, 'Six Inches from the Presidency: The Gary Hart Jokes as Public Opinion', *Western Folklore*, Vol. 48, No. 1, January 1989, pp. 43-51.
11. His dislike for broccoli was genuine. First Lady Barbara Bush graciously met a delegation from the United Fresh Fruit & Vegetable Association on the South Lawn at the White House in 1990. The association made a donation of 10,000 lbs of broccoli 'in the president's good name' to a community food bank, calling it a 'green beam' in Bush's much derided talk of a 'Thousand Points of Light'. See youtube.com/watch?v=SoLIy5icDLo in which broccoli fan

Barbara Bush, a highly popular First Lady, says 'I'm gonna tell you the honest truth, the president is never gonna eat broccoli'.

12. Richard Cohen, 'The Execution of Rickey Ray Rector', *The Washington Post*, 23/2/1993.

13. Jacob Weisberg, *George W. Bushisms* (New York: Fireside, 2001), p. 76.

14. *Texas Death Row: Last Words. Last Meals. Last Rites*, edited by Bill Crawford (London: Penguin Books, 2008), p. 400. Singer-songwriter Steve Earle, an anti-death penalty campaigner, was a witness to the execution.

15. Sasha Johnson, 'High schoolers pitch hardballs at McCain', edition.cnn.com/2007/POLITICS/09/04/mccain.question/index.html.

16. Dan Balz and Haynes Johnson, *The Battle for America: The Story of an Extraordinary Election* (New York: Penguin Books, 2010), p. 372. The reference is to Johnson (Texas) winning in 1964, Carter (Georgia) in 1976 and Clinton (Arkansas) in 1992 and 1996.

17. Trump's winning margins in Michigan, Wisconsin and Pennsylvania add up to a total of 77,744 votes.

18. Nolan D. McCaskill, 'Trump accuses Cruz's father of helping JFK's assassin', politico.com, 5/3/2016.

19. Jonathan Allen and Amie Parnes, *Shattered: Inside Hillary Clinton's Doomed Campaign* (New York: Crown, 2017), p. 356.

20. Maggie Haberman, 'Trump, Lifelong New Yorker, Declares Himself a Resident of Florida', nytimes.com, 31/10/2019, updated 4/11/2019.

Conclusion: Election Night: By the Dawn's Early Light

1. Dark-horse candidate Polk's 'first major decision was crucial: to declare for a one-term presidency' and convince miffed rivals in key electoral states 'that he meant it', John Seigenthaler, *James K. Polk* (New York: Times Books, 2004), p. 92.

2. In the antebellum (pre-Civil War) era, which stands out for its poor and single-term presidents, historians regard Polk as a rare success.

3. Charlie Cook, 'Biden May Be One and Done Regardless of Whether He Makes A Pledge', *The Cook Political Report*, 1/5/2020.

4. 'Lessons from stone: The last driller of Mount Rushmore,' *The Economist*, 3/8/2019, p. 31. The National Park Service excellent website, nps.gov, says that FDR spoke at the 1936 dedication of Jefferson, who was the second face unveiled (joining Washington). Lincoln and Teddy Roosevelt were dedicated in 1937 and 1939, respectively.

5. 'That Berning feeling: What does Bernie Sanders's political revolution hope to accomplish?', *The Economist*, 29/2/2020. Danville Post Office was officially renamed in honour of Vermont native and anti-slavery campaigner Thaddeus Stevens, and Fair Haven Post Office after prominent native Matthew Lyon who backed Jefferson following the 1800 Electoral College tie.

6. Lewis L. Gould, *1968: The Election That Changed America* (Chicago: Ivan R. Dee, 1993), p. 6.

7. Providing the seven faithless electors had kept in line which is more likely with an actual winner at stake though others may have been naughty instead.

8. Richard Hofstadter, *The American Political Tradition* (New York: Alfred A. Knopf, 1979), 25th anniversary edition, p. 42.

9. Estimates for deaths in the U.S. Civil War range from 620,000 to the more recent 750,000.

10. bioguideretro.congress.gov/Home/MemberDetails?memIndex=h000821. O'Daniel is satirised in the Coen brothers' 2000 film *O Brother, Where Art Thou?* with George Clooney. Also see Seth Shepard McKay, *W. Lee O'Daniel and Texas Politics, 1938-1942* (Texas Tech Press, 1944).

11. Bill Crawford, *Please Pass The Biscuits, Pappy* (Austin: University of Texas Press, 2004), p. 45. The book's dust jacket says O'Daniel 'decided to run for (Texas) governor in 1938 as a way to sell more flour'.

12. As of 1 June 2020 the four living former presidents are Jimmy Carter (b. 1924), Bill Clinton (b. 1946), George W. Bush (b. 1946) and Barack Obama (b. 1961). Readers who email the author to say they just saw Abraham Lincoln stocking up on toilet paper in their local Co-op will not get a reply.
13. bbc.co.uk/news/election-us-2016-37885746.
14. uselectionatlas.org/INFORMATION/ARTICLES/Election Night2016/pe2016elecnighttime.php. For his website alone, Leip deserves to be at least vice president.
15. See from 12:54 in youtube.com/watch?v=iiBg7JbcYqA.
16. 'Sixty-four-year-old lands in field after grabbing ejection handle to steady himself, French air investigators find', theguardian.com/world/2020/apr/14/man-accidentally-ejects-himself-from-fighter-jet-during-surprise-flight.
17. A rival campaign to 'Make America Normal Again' is also underway.
18. AOC may have to wait a while for a Senate vacancy in New York with Senate Minority Leader Chuck Schumer, 69, not going anywhere. 'The most dangerous place in Washington is between Schumer and a TV camera' goes one famous joke attributed to Bob Dole. Kirsten Gillibrand, the junior senator for New York, is only in her 50s. The oldest-ever U.S. senator is former segregationist Strom Thurmond of South Carolina at 100.
19. nbcnews.com/politics/meet-the-press/new-electoral-map-comes-focus-ahead-2020-census-n1110546.
20. D. W. Brogan, *The American Problem* (London: Hamish Hamilton, 1944), p. 133. His equally talented son, Hugh Brogan, wrote *The Penguin History of the United States of America* (London: Penguin Books, 1990). The Monroe Doctrine, which only acquired its name after Monroe's presidency had ended, warned other nations not to mess about with Latin America. Father Brogan's anecdote was included in my classic *Always on a Sunday: An Englishman in Greece* (Athens: Athens News, 2006), now disgracefully out of print. Acknowledgements

Acknowledgements

Huge thanks to writers over the centuries - professors, journalists, gossips – who have left such a rich legacy for American history readers. They have done a great country proud.

Praise also to Wolves fan Connor Stait and misguided Arsenal supporter Alex Bennett, my able editors at Amberley Publishing.

A 2020 election guide likely appearing in 2021 is an unusual marketing ploy but I am entirely to blame. Watch out for my 2024 predictions in late 2025.

It was still a rush to finish. Spotted a mistake? Mark your own book and keep it to yourself.

Brian Church
Shrewsbury, England